Prescription for an Exciting Love Life

This is a relationship book using a love story to illustrate —and provide the essentials for— lasting love. It presents guidelines to help everyone avoid the pitfalls that ruin long-lasting commitment for a romantic life.

Jean Daniel François, M.D.

Copyright 2010 by Jean Daniel François, MD
G.O.A.L, Inc.
1713–19 Ralph Avenue
Brooklyn, New York 11236
Phone: 718–531–6100
Fax 718–531–2329

All rights reserved solely by the author. No part of this book may be reproduced or transmitted in any form or by any means, electronic or mechanical, including photocopying, recording, e-booking, or by any information storage and retrieval system without the express written permission of the author.

Printed in the United States of America
First Edition
Cover concept and design: Denise Gibson
ISBN: 978-0-9823142-4-1

Also by Jean Daniel François, M.D.

Prescription for a Successful Life

Les Clés de la Réussite Authentique

Prescription for a Successful Career in Medicine

Through The Light of Sola Scriptura

You may visit the authors website, www.successfullife.us or email him at jfranc6704@gmail.com.

For any information, please write:

>Jean Daniel François, MD
>P.O. Box 360543
>Brooklyn, NY 11236
>U.S.A.
>
>Phone (718)531–6100
>Fax (718)531–2329
>Email: jfranc6704@gmail.com
>
>www.successfullife.us

Acknowledgments

I have had the distinct privilege of encountering many talented and sincere people who gave me wise and practical advice. Their valuable inputs have helped me tremendously. Words are unable to truly express my gratitude towards all of them. I am also indebted to all of those who have written and spoken about such a popular topic before me. I hope they can see themselves through the ideas and words of this book. I am not able to cite all of them. I must acknowledge the skills and selfless devotion of Claudia Joseph, who provided the indispensable youthful and sensitive woman's touch. I am grateful for the enthusiasm and dedication of Clarajine Thibaud and Emlynn Beauzil for their contributions in editing the manuscript. I am thankful to my daughter, Sarah, and my son, Jean Daniel, who offered ideas to make the book more appropriate for a young audience.

Disclaimer

Neither this book nor any other material by the author, Jean Daniel François, MD, is intended to replace a personal coach or adviser. Everyone's situation is different and requires a unique approach tailored to their specific needs. The primary goal of this book is to make people aware of their own condition and to take steps to improve their love life in order to have an exciting, meaningful, and dynamic relationship with their partner. Neither the author nor the publisher shall be held responsible or judged liable to any person or institution for any loss, disappointment, or damage attributed directly or indirectly to the ideas expressed in this book. Should you discover any error that may have inadvertently slipped in, please contact the author. Thanks!

About the Author

Dr. Jean Daniel François is a practicing physician who is on a mission to cause change in people's lives in various domains. He is the author of a few books, including Prescription for a Successful Life, Prescription For a Successful Career in Medicine, Les Clés de la Réussite Authentique, Through the Light of Sola Scriptura. He is a leading authority and public speaker on personal motivation, family counseling, health, spirituality, family life, and domestic violence. He is well liked and appreciated in the communities where he speaks.

This book is dedicated to all of those who have ever experienced love or who are bound to fall in love.

Preface

LOVE!

It's a word that most of us have used at different times in our lives. But how many of us know its true meaning anyway? What is love?

Love is an inherent, intense, positive, and emotional feeling of affection that can be experienced in various ways and in different domains. Love flourishes in our hearts, and we experience it even before birth. From the cradle to the grave, we are aware of experiencing either authentic love or its absence. Our entire life revolves around it.

As our world evolves, is there any real love out there?

Can anyone be trusted to love? Whatever previous opinions you may have had, whatever experiences you have lived through, I want to invite you to come along with me and make this simple journey.

If you needed a brain surgeon, would you choose someone without the proper training? If you were traveling, would you feel comfortable with a rookie pilot and no copilot? Shouldn't the same be true for our love lives?

We need to learn how to love. We need to know some basic principles about love, because love is such a vital part of our lives. All of us have some ideas about it, but not too many know the essentials of a lasting relationship.

I wrote this book especially for you. To engage your interest, I spiced it up a little, but not too much—just enough to keep you interested in it until the last page. Are you in love? Read it! Do you feel loved? Read it! Do you feel betrayed? Read It! Are you struggling with a relationship? Read it! Are you about to start a relationship? You still need to read it. Are you thinking about throwing in the towel? Read it! My only hope is that when you are done reading it, you will have a better grasp of how to begin and maintain a healthy relationship.

As you already know, love is a vast concept that is involved in almost everything we think, see, or do. Grasping the entire subject in one book would be foolhardy. The focus instead is on relationships between two partners who choose to share their lives with each other. This is both a challenging and an inspiring journey.

1

It was a partly-cloudy, hot and humid summer Sunday evening. Dad was out of town at a conference, Mom went to church for a social gathering, and Sophia's brother was driving all over town, as usual. This was the best time for Sophia to catch up on her reading.

She sat by one of the windows in the living room in her Dad's favorite chair, her feet on a small table, while listening to some light classical music; she started reading Kate Chopin's *The Awakening*. The phone rang. Sophia ignored it as usual. It kept ringing, but to no avail. She had a good reason not to answer it: anyone close to her or the family would know all of their cell phone numbers. It had to be one of those people with nothing better to do on a Sunday afternoon than to bother decent, peaceful citizens. The phone continued, as if begging to be picked up. Concentration broken, Sophia braced herself, dropped a bookmark into the book, got up slowly, and picked up the phone. In a soft but annoyed voice, she answered, ready to send the intruder away.

"Hello, Marcels' residence!"

"Hi, my name is Kevin; may I speak to Sophia, please?"

"This is she. How may I help you?"

At the other end the voice is a bit hesitant and somewhat tremulous. After a short pause, the young man continued

"Well, you may not remember me, but you and I went to elementary school together…"

"Really?" interrupted Sophia, slightly interested.

"…Then we lost track of each other. My parents moved out of state, where I went to junior high and high school. Later on I joined the military. I just got back from my tour in the war, and I'm trying to settle down. Your name is still stuck in my mind, so I decided to give you a call."

"How interesting! By the way, how did you get my number?"

"It's a long story. I don't want to impose on you, but why don't we meet and talk about it and catch up? Name the time and place at your convenience, or if you want I can stop by your house."

Sophia remained silent for a while (trying to quickly calculate how many days it would take to go on a crash diet, get her hair done…).

"Hello? Sophia, are you there?" asked Kevin.

"Yes! I'm here. How about two or three weeks from now?"

"Two weeks? Can't you squeeze me into your schedule in the next day or so?"

"Absolutely not!"

"How about two days?"

"I am sorry, I can't. We haven't seen each other in eight years. You've waited this long; you're not going to die if you wait another week or two."

"Believe me, I might. Anything is possible."

Sophia remembered her mother's advice: "As a lady,

never reveal that you are too eager to meet someone who may be interested in you. You do not want him to think you are either too easy or looking for adventure." So she composed herself and said:

"Listen Kevin, why don't you give me your phone number? I'll check my schedule and I will get back to you as soon as possible."

"OK! That's fair enough. I'll be waiting for your call."

Kevin gave Sophia his phone number and his e-mail address. Her cell phone was charging in her room, so she quickly wrote the information down on a piece of paper for the time being. They said goodbye and hung-up.

Sophia was intrigued. She kept searching and searching her memory, but remained clueless. She remembered vaguely that in the early months of elementary school there were three Kevins in her class. The girls distinguished them by adding the boy's second initial after the Kevin: Kevin B was bright and very articulate; Kevin S was silly and childish; and Kevin F was funny, chubby and short. Which one could this be?

She tried to recall those days. She remembered the neighborhood, the classrooms, where she used to sit, the teachers, the playgrounds. She remembered how the girls used to gather together, and the boys used to tease them. She even remembered one girl, Caroline, whose hair some boy glued to the desk while she was sleeping. It had to be cut to get her unattached. She still saw Miss Barney, her math teacher, who told her she would never be good at math. How she wished she could see her now with straight A's from an Ivy League university. She remembered the music teacher who was mean to her and discouraged her from furthering her studies in voice and piano. She also had good memories of so many outstanding teachers and the ever-present elementary school principal. She still could not remember who Kevin was-or any of the three Kevins for that matter. After agonizing for a while about it, she decided to call Lakisha for help.

"Hey Kisha, guess what?"

"What's up Sophia, you sound pleasantly puzzled?"

"I just received one of the weirdest phone calls in my life."

"What is it? You won a million dollars!"

"Stop being silly! Someone named Kevin called me and wanted to meet with me."

"Wow! Maybe he saw you on MySpace. Who's the guy?

"I have no idea. He said he went to school with me. Do you remember a Kevin in elementary school?"

"I know we had three, that much I can recall too. But I don't remember any of them."

"When are you going to see him?" Lakisha asked.

"Are you out of your mind? What if this guy is a lunatic, a crazy sex offender, serial killer…?"

"Hold your horses Sophia! You are not marrying him or taking him home. He just wants to meet with you. He could also be a gentleman who always had a crush on you and who is still interested. What have you got to lose?"

"My life is on the line here," replied Sophia.

"Come on Sophia! Ask him to meet you in 'the Village' right inside the Starbucks, by the precinct. That way you will feel secure and I'll tell our friends from campus to be on the lookout. Meet with him tomorrow and see what this is all about and then move on."

"I have 2 previous appointments."

"OK! Suit yourself, my dear."

"I need to be mentally and physically prepared."

"Ha-ha-ha! In that case, it will take a century."

"Lakisha!"

"I'm only kidding."

"—OK! I'll get back to you."

"Bye Sophia!"

While Sophia was talking to Lakisha in her room, Sophia's mother came home. She cleaned up the entire house, picking-up every scrap of paper left out and throwing it in the trash. She put out the trash for the Sanitation Department to pick up in morning.

Sophia told her mother about the call. They agreed she should meet with Kevin at her convenience and not read anymore into it than just someone who is a bit bored and is trying to reconnect with old friends. She went back to her room, but since she couldn't sleep, she decided to go through her dresser drawers, where she stumbled upon an old diary. She opened it and saw an old letter from her Dad.

Florida, July 15

My Beloved Daughter,

It is 9 PM; as usual I am in my hotel room while my colleagues are out at a restaurant. I am thinking about the family, thinking about my beloved daughter.

I assume at this time you are watching some scary movie or 'Law and Order' or even sleeping. At sixteen, you definitely have plenty on your mind: high school, a career, and your looks, peer pressure, your parent's expectations and your obligations to them, and love. However I know you are well equipped to get the most out of this world. You have enough discernment to know how and when to take life seriously, enough common sense to enjoy the ride while on your journey to reach your set goals. I would like to remind you of the seven key factors your future depends on:

1. *Environment*
2. *Judgment and level of maturity*
3. *Choices*
4. *Actions and decisions*
5. *Responsibility and discipline*
6. *Results and consequences*
7. *Attitude*

Let me also point out that the ability to love, learn, and behave appropriately defines us and affects our life cycle. Remember these six key factors that reflect such ability:

1. Character: *it shines through trials and tribulations as well as in triumph and glory. It includes values and moral courage that does not change based on time and circumstances.*

2. Attitude: *it remains positive rain or shine. It is proactive and never allows people or circumstances to poison it.*

3. Commitment and loyalty in the midst of stormy situations: *it includes sterling honesty and perseverance.*

4. Altruism and gratitude: *a sense of duty to help others in their time of need, and the ability to be thankful and grateful for others' help.*

5. Humility and simplicity: *no one loves the company of a peacock who is always bragging about his prowess.*

6. Talents: *skills along with discipline will take you beyond your imagination.*

Finally, this is also the time when your love blossoms, overcomes you, and wants to own you. Because you are young, beautiful, and bright, there will be many young folks who will come after you. I believe they may have tried already. You too may feel some great attraction toward one or two. But always ask yourself why? What do they want? I am convinced the day will come when your heart will start pounding, your mouth will become dry, your head will be foggy, and your entire body will melt under the power of love. However, be patient and remember the aforementioned attributes.

The other day you asked me, "Dad, how do you know you are in love? How did you know Mom was the one?" The answer was simple: when the right one comes you will know it. You will know it by the way you feel toward him. You will know it by the way he looks at you, the way he talks to you, the way he cares about you, the way he wants to protect you, the way he wants to always share your company, the way he treats you in private as well as in public, and the way he allows you to grow and be yourself. Look into his eyes; they are the mirror to his soul. Love is more than a sudden electrical feeling that rushes through your entire body. It must take into consideration a few factors, including the personal characteristics mentioned above. Many define love as an outburst of a flame, a blind, selfish emotion. They feel it is a temporary excitement that lives as long as one night—or a sensual passion, an earthly amusement with gateways highly visited. However, people with experience will tell you that love is more than just a fling. The fountain of love covers all aspects of life. Seek to find a lasting love. This is everyone's challenge. This is yours too, my love. Again, when you find it, you will know. You must never forget that there are many imitations. So be yourself, be confident, and have the right attitude.

I will see you soon. In the meantime, keep up the good spirits.

Love always,

Dad

Sophia was a bit amused and puzzled. "Strange coincidence", she thought. She put everything back in her drawers and went to bed.

Despite the weather forecast, Monday turned out to be a beautiful sunny day with mild temperatures: the sky was tinged with blue and pinkish spots. Although she went to bed at a reasonable hour, Sophia was restless most of the night. She finally fell asleep around five in the morning and woke up at eight. She went downstairs to the kitchen to get her book and the paper where she had written Kevin's number. It was nowhere to be found. She figured Kevin would call again. Most of the day went by without her doing much. Days and weeks passed by, and life went on with its normal activities.

Labor Day weekend is a busy period for all. Schools are opening and parents are sending their kids to school for the first time. Some are still looking for a school that will accept their precious pearls; others are still trying to make ends meet and are facing daily challenges.

Sophia was excited. A long-time friend was getting married in Canada, and Sophia was to be one of the bridesmaids. Initially her parents were opposed to her driving. But between all the clothes and the wedding gift, she had so much to transport that they finally agreed to let her use their car and drive alone to Quebec for the wedding. That Friday night, traffic was particularly heavy, and it was pouring. Sophia wanted everything to be in order for the great wedding that her friend deserved. Lost in her thoughts, Sophia skidded into someone else's car from behind. The accident wasn't serious. It was no big deal, just a little fender bender.

Sophia, however, was shaking like a leaf. The other driver—a gentleman—got out and looked at both their cars. There seemed to be nothing damaged except for a small scratch on the young man's bumper. Upon learning that she was fine, without even looking at her face, and preoccupied with his cell phone conversation, he disappeared into the traffic with not so much as a glance. Sophia continued on her way, but a bit slower this time, until she made it to her destination. Throughout the remainder of the drive, she kept thinking about that accident; it was her first. There was something unique about the driver of the other vehicle, something that seemed familiar. She hadn't had time to ask any questions, and they had not even exchanged names or insurance information. She was really puzzled and kept searching through her memory. But no answer came.

After all the excitement, and the interminable preparations, the wedding ceremony was a great success. Everyone was happy.

At the reception, on her way to the ladies' room, she saw him out of the corner of her eye. This time she recognized him. It was the young man from the highway. After freshening up in the ladies' room, she hurried out hoping to catch up with him in the reception hall. But when she came out, he was nowhere to be found. She looked in vain through all the other halls. In a panic, she ran to the parking lot and saw him speeding out. She ran right in front of his car. Had he not known how to use his brakes properly and quickly, she could have been history.

This time he had no choice but to come out and talk.

"Wait a minute, aren't you that lady who hit my car on the highway?"

"Yes and I wanted to come and apologize to you." She spoke in a childish tone.

"I could have hit you!"

"I took my chances."

They both laughed. It was raining hard. Her lovely hair was getting wet and so was her beautiful dress. He invited her into his car in order to continue the conversation.

"You're crazy," he blurted.

"Is that the first thing you say when you meet a person?"

"So tell me, what is your name?"

"My name is Sophia Marcel."

"Sophia!" He laughed. "I can't believe this!"

"What's so funny?"

He was laughing so hard he was gasping for air.

"I bet you don't remember me."

"I am sorry, but I do not. I have met quite a few people in my life, and I don't remember all of them, do you?"

"I am sorry, I don't blame you, but you and I once were in the same class way, way back."

Sophia became less guarded. "Really! Come to think of it you sound a bit familiar. But believe me, I can't figure it out right now."

"That's okay. I can understand how an attractive young woman like you may not remember someone like me—"

"Oh no, I did not mean to make it sound like that. These days, people use all kinds of lines to start a conversation—"

"Forgive me, but you can't blame them. A rare beauty like you is a challenge even for a holy man."

"Thank you! So, you are one of the guys I went to school with many years ago."

"You got it right, madam!"

"Really? What was the name of that school?"

"Well, you and I went to pre-K and kindergarten and we even shared some elementary classes in our neighborhood in Brooklyn."

"What neighborhood was that, may I ask?"

"East Flatbush. I do not remember the exact name—"

"Is your name Kevin?"

"Yes! So you remember me, don't you?"

"Wow! You changed! You are not so—"

"Fat. Don't be afraid to say it. You and I remember how kids used to call me Kevin F—F for funny in front of me and F for fat behind my back."

"I am sorry Kevin—"

"No need to apologize! You can't believe how bad it was when I got to junior and high school. I joined the football team; there was an incentive to be heavy and big. Almost everybody forgot my real name and called me Frigidaire because I was always looking into it to find something to eat."

"You look pretty fit now," Sophia said.

"I enrolled in college but I left after a year.

"I wanted to join the army like my dad, but I was too heavy. Our next door neighbor had a fitness center, and he saw my dilemma. He took me under his wing, and in six months I met all the requirements to get into the army. In basic training, I became even more disciplined, with regular exercise and a healthy diet. Now I'm five-eleven and 170 pounds of solid muscle. That's one of the reasons I'm grateful to the U.S. military. They give you discipline, a sense of purpose and the ability to fly with your own two wings. Anyway, what a strange way for us to meet after all these years!"

"I must confess, Sophia—please forgive me for saying this—I am really attracted to you. I always have been."

"Kevin, there is more to a relationship than just physical

attractiveness. You've just finished telling me how you're a much different person as an adult than you were as a child. Well, the same may be true for me. You really don't know me at all. So you may be attracted to what you imagine me to be, but you can't know whether you're really attracted to me as I am."

"Sophia, please forgive me; I know how I feel. Now that I see you again, I do not want to miss the chance of telling you how much I love you; even if it is too late, you have the right to know. This is not a kid's fantasy. I can't hide such strong feelings anymore. Do you have any idea how heavy the burden of being consumed by love is? I can't miss the opportunity to confess it. I cannot bear this burden anymore. I love you. I have never been great with words. I just wish you could see my mind, my heart; even then you could barely have a glimpse of the intensity of my love for you. I used to fantasize about how you look, what you could be doing. Now that my eyes have seen you, I must confess to you, you are ten times more beautiful than the way I used to imagine you."

"But Kevin…"

"Look at you, Sophia. Wow! I could never have imagined that you were going to become such a gorgeous young woman.
I am so proud to meet the real Miss Universe!"

Kevin looked around and noticed that the weather had improved. "Even Mother Nature is on your side. Everywhere I've gone lately, it was raining. But now that I see you, all of a sudden the rain stops, the stars are shining; the birds are singing—you bring spring at the end of summer. You are fantastic. Heaven knows how happy I am to see you again. From the time I left town until now, my heart has been wrapped, clipped, put in a brown bag and dumped into a dark drawer. But now I that see you, oh what a miracle! I am alive again!"

"Don't you think you have said enough to a woman who may be married, may have children…?" Sophia interrupted.

Kevin replied in a pleading voice, "I meant everything I said. There is no shame in telling someone how much you love her, if you mean it and are willing to pay the price and start the journey until you conquer her heart."

"What if her heart is already conquered?"

"Then, you dethrone the current conqueror!" He went on to add "In the war of love, all bets are off, all means are acceptable, and no measures are too strong. Everything is worth the ultimate price and the means are justified by the result obtained; the rules vary with the targeted price to win. As the number of challenges increase, as the number of peril augment, they serve to strengthen the ultimate winner."

Sophia laughed and said, "You see love as a war to win. You are just plain crazy."

Kevin was mesmerized by her smile. Her bright teeth were framed by lips that looked like a rose about to open to the sun's rays on a spring day. The car radio was playing You Light Up My Life in the background'

"Sophia, what are your plans for the remaining hours of this fortunate day?"

Sophia pursed her lips, planted her toes deep on the floor, took her eyes off Kevin and said, "Oh, I have so much to do and so little time to do it. I must return home in less than twelve hours. I need to catch up with work."

"Can't you please give us an hour together? We could go someplace, a movie, a play; take a walk, or anything you want. I just would love to spend some more time with you, Sophia."

"I am flattered, Kevin, but not now; another time, at another place."

"I understand," said Kevin. "I, too, have to go to a meeting tonight. When both of us get back to town, please let us meet again. I have enjoyed your company and I would love to share more of it. Can we meet Tuesday night at eight? Where do you usually like to go?"

"What can I say! I'll get back to you on that—I am late. Bye!" She opened the door and walked a few feet.

"Bye, Sophia!"

"Bye, Kevin!"

"Tuesday night at eight, please?"

Sophia did not answer. As they shook hands, Kevin knelt and kissed her right hand. Kevin walked slowly back to his car. Sophia walked back to the reception, which was about to end. She did not look back.

Somehow, deep inside, Sophia felt Kevin was genuine. But she did not want to get into something she was not sure about. She needed to know more about him. She thanked God she did not tell him she shared some of the same feelings that were eating him alive. She thought, *Mom and Dad would be really proud of me!*

Kevin could not go anywhere. He sat in his car, as if he had forgotten how to start it. He watched as she disappeared into the crowd. He tried to compose himself. Things were too weird for him. Since the day he spoke to Sophia over the phone, he had not stopped dreaming about her. He had been thinking about her all the time. When he thought she did not care to see him, out of the blue, she popped up and knocked his socks off. "Why, for heavens' sake did I have to see her again today? Why did I have to let her go? I wish I knew how to convince her about how I really feel," Kevin said to himself out loud. "My mother told me once that women have a way of seeing things through your eyes, your voice, your handshakes and your goodbyes, and I hope she is right." Before he met Sophia, he had a vague idea about her. But now that he had seen her, he could not believe his eyes. She was far more beautiful than he had ever imagined. She was wearing a simple silver tunic with a V in the front and back, covered with a see-through overblouse. It showed off her hourglass figure, sustaining her well-proportioned bust line and gently pressed the hips. *What a fantastic figure! What an elegant lady. She has an ideal body and a great personality. When she walks, what a symphony! Her entire being is in harmony. What an aura! Wow! Mama Mia!* Kevin threw both fists up through the sunroof as if to punch the air.

Kevin appeared calm on the outside, while inside he felt like a race car going 100 miles per hour. *This is too good to be true.*

He began to review his twenty-five years of existence, especially the last five. He remembered how he felt when he was in college and fell in love with Pat. She too was beautiful. She too made him happy. The two of them planned a wonderful life together. Then one morning a classmate went into a shooting rampage and killed Pat. Kevin was devastated. He joined the army shortly after. As he reminisced, his eyes filled with tears he could not hold back. A passerby blew his horn so hard that it startled Kevin back to reality.

> He caught himself repeating, "Oh no, this is not going to happen again! Oh no!
>
> Wait a minute; I do not know much about Sophia. This is a girl I knew in elementary school. She is so attractive and beautiful. I am sure guys must always be hitting on her. What if—? Is she engaged or married? I saw no wedding ring, or did I? Is she not interested?"

She gave him no specific hints that could encourage him. He missed his best opportunity: just him and her. So many things he could have told her. But his thoughts were so dense and were coming all at once, he was not sure he said anything to impress her. He thought that he blew it. Kevin said to himself, *Kevin, Kevin, Kevin, you did it again*. You always mess up. Kevin kept wondering *what if*—as he drove back to his hotel. It was just a couple of miles away, but heavy traffic held him up for twenty minutes. Desperate, he made an illegal U-turn to go back to talk to Sophia.

Sophia, after giving her best wishes to the married couple and her friends, felt so drained. She went back to where she was staying to get some rest. When she got there she had so much on her mind, she decided to call her friend Lakisha and her mother to vent a little. Then she emailed her dad, who quickly replied:

> *Sept 3*
>
> *My Beloved Daughter,*
>
> *I just read your email with great interest. From what I gathered, you seem to a date with someone new on Tuesday. Parents always hope this one*

*will be the one. I know you know what to do..
Nevertheless, please allow me to remind you of a few
key points, just in case you need reinforcement.*

*1. The idea of dating cannot be taken lightly. You
should know something about a person you go out
on a date with. Going on a date with a perfect
stranger is never a wise decision. This is why so-
called cyber dating is not generally advisable. In
your situation you have what you might call an
appointment, but that would be too formal, too
business like. Perhaps we should say you have a
rendezvous, or you have arranged to meet with
someone. But because somehow I feel there is
some romantic intent, let's say you have a date;
you have arranged to go out socially with Kevin.*

*2. Having a date with someone assumes you know
something about that person and you are going
out with him on one occasion. It is different
from dating that person. Dating underscores
the idea of an ongoing romantic relationship
exclusively between two people who want to
get to know each other better and determine
whether or not they can ultimately commit
to each other for a lasting conjugal life.*

*A decision to continue seeing that person means
you think the relationship must be worth
pursuing. The decision should hinge on honesty
and freedom to decide with mutual respect*

*Dating goes through some stages: some level of
bilateral friendship; going out once or twice; going
out steadily; getting engaged in order to tie the knot.*

Why do people date? They date because:

a. *It is an opportunity to be social; it is a part of life to interact with others. Going out with other people, especially in a group, helps build character.*

b. *It gives people the chance to learn about others, including members of the opposite sex.*

c. *People want to fulfill the normal yearning to love and be loved.*

d. *They want to learn about each other and decide whether or not this is an activity that is worth pursuing with that particular individual.*

e. *They sincerely hope they will wind up having a lasting relationship with one another.*

It is worth pointing out that there are some wrong reasons for dating, including these:

a. *Doing it because everybody is engaged in the activity; in other words, peer pressure.*

b. *To amuse oneself and conquer as many hearts as possible and put them in your conquest list.*

Reaching an appropriate age and a reasonable level of maturity are required for dating.

Preparation for the first date

Remember that the first impression counts. So:

1. Be yourself and try not to appear too nervous. Get some good rest. Choose your clothes and shoes carefully by taking into account your best image, your comfort, your body type, the season, the occasion and the place where you may be going.

2. *Do some basic homework: take time to get an idea about current events, sports scores and ratings, etc.*

3. *Avoid being too flashy, such as with excessive lipstick or makeup, and come up with a proper hair style. Control your manners: Don't chew bubble gum; pay attention to how and where you bend down, to avoid exposing yourself; and keep a straight posture.*

4. *Watch both your verbal and nonverbal messages.*

5. *Practice your listening skills and your way of smiling, your tone and the pitch of your voice.*

6. *Do not set your expectations too high. Take it as it comes with your mind set on what is acceptable and what is not acceptable.*

During the actual date

1. *Avoid being late or too early. (Tardiness may be a sign of lack of interest or lack of discipline, or may show that you are unable to keep track of time; being too early may convey the wrong message, including being desperate).*

2. *Give a warm greeting and smile naturally, while keeping good eye contact.*

3. *Be observant: notice his outfit, level of cleanliness, alertness, enthusiasm in meeting you, and his manners.*

4. Remember he may be shy and nervous, too. Try not to overshadow him. Give him a chance to express himself.

5. Find a tactful way to learn of the plans for the night, if he fails to tell you.

6. Keep a clear mind and avoid alcohol or any drugs.

7. Know the boundaries and stand your ground without being boring or cold.

After that first date, he may or may not ask you out again. If he does, your answer depends on how the first date went. Of course there are exceptions to the rule.

Six key ways to know if you should go out with him again:

1. Self-image: personal appearance, punctuality, cleanliness, sobriety, fund of knowledge, level of maturity, stability, and reliability. Is he natural or flaky?

2. The way he treats you and greets you: did he bring you flowers? Where does he plan to go and what does he plan to do? Does he bother to tell you? Does he care to know whether or not you are beside him or far behind him while walking? In the restaurant, does he let you choose anything you want or does he want to dictate to you what to choose. Does he let you choose your own drink? If you do not like what you selected, look at his facial expression. How does he look and what does he say when he gets the bill? Does he ask you to pay for the meal; does he ask you to lend him some money? How does he react if something clumsy happens? Does he love to hear himself talk in continuous monologue or does he listen to you? Does he care to know your viewpoint about the way he plans the evening? Does he care about what you like or dislike? What kind of language does he use? How much does he talk about himself? What are his manners: does he like to touch a lot?

3. *His table manners, how fast he eats, whether or not he talks with his mouth full; do you see the food while it is being masticated inside his mouth? And how much does he eat? This may give you a quick preview of the overall family situation.*

4. *Communication: verbal and body language.*

5. *How he reacts when you catch him off guard by asking him a controversial question on a topic such as politics, religion, discrimination, or sexual orientation. Does he have a sense of humor? Does he know how to disagree civilly or does he want to fight and win at any cost?*

6. *Does he have values and ethical principles that guide his life? Does he believe in anything, anyone?*

You get my drift.

Love always,

Dad

3

Kevin could not wait for the upcoming meeting. Every minute seemed to last an eternity. Finally, the day came and Kevin arrived at their agreed location a half-hour early. He got himself a special waiter solely at the service of himself and Sophia. He wanted everything to be perfect: food, music, décor. As the clock marked 8:00, he waited eagerly to see Sophia. He waited until 8:30, 9:00, 9:30, and until 10:00, and still Sophia was nowhere in sight. Finally, Kevin picked himself up and left for home. He was both furious and perplexed. What is wrong with Sophia? She is nice, beautiful, and physically attractive. Everything looks great, but something is definitely wrong. He called her at home; nobody answered. He called her cell phone, she had turned it off. Kevin began to review the interactions with Sophia. He said to himself, unless she has a good explanation, she is definitely not interested. Maybe she was just trying to be polite and had never liked him.

Discouraged and annoyed, he threw himself onto his bed, but sleep refused to come to his rescue. He tossed and turned. Finally, at 11: 25 he turned on the TV and saw a news summary. Among the local headlines: a big fire in Brooklyn. He turned it off and pulled the covers over his head. The night was not kind to him. He had a few nightmares about the war he had just left. At 9:00 the next morning, his phone rang. It was Sophia:

"Hi Kevin. Sorry I could not make it last night."

"What happened?" he asked nonchalantly.

"Oh! You didn't know?"

"What?" asked Kevin while fixing up his bed.

"My house was on fire last night."

"Oh no! Is everybody all right?" Kevin took a serious tone.

"My dad had to go to the hospital for smoke inhalation. But he is OK now."

"What about the house?"

"Only a small part, where most of Dad's paintings were, was destroyed by smoke."

"I am sorry to hear that. I will see you soon."

Kevin belonged to a group of people who believe that when other people are in distress or hard times, there need not be an invitation to go and visit. So without asking whether or not he should come, he showed up at Sophia's home. It was a modest three-bedroom home, with an open porch that led into a sizable, well-illuminated, L-shaped living room. There was a full dining room, a well-equipped kitchen with one door leading into the basement and another door that took you up to the second floor, where the bedrooms were. The house itself looked small on the outside; it was surrounded by trees, plants, and flowers in addition to a well-kept lawn. The lot covered about 6,500 square feet.

His heart began pounding as he approached the door. He stood there immobile. He did not have the courage to ring the bell. He started talking to himself: "Am I doing the right thing? What if—" As he was about to leave, the door opened.

"Excuse me sir, did you ring the bell?" asked a middle aged woman.

Kevin stood there speechless.

"Sir, are you ok?"

"Oh yes. Excuse me, is this Sophia's residence? I would like to see her."

"Come on in" said the woman. This is the Marcel residence. Sophia does live here and I am her mother, Bertha. Is she expecting you?"

"Not really. Is she in?" Kevin asked while trying to control his tremors and hide his perspiration.

"Excuse the appearance and the smell. Part of our house caught fire last night; that is why everything seems so upside down."

"That is terrible! Sophia told me about it briefly this morning. So I wanted to find out how everyone was doing. How is her dad doing? Is he ok? Is there anything I can do for you folks?"

"Mr. Marcel is much better, thank you. Please sit down. You just missed Sophia. She went to get something from the pharmacy. She will be right back. Make yourself at home. Would you care for something to drink?"

"No thanks," replied Kevin even though his stomach was growling.

Bertha sat two chairs away from him. She noticed that he was still shaking a bit and sweating. The silence was loud and heavy, while each one was caught up in his or her own thoughts.

"What is your name? Are you a good friend of Sophia's?"

"I'm Kevin."

"Kevin!" Bertha chuckled. "Are you the one I spoke to last week? How nice of you to come!"

She reached out and shook his hand again, as if to tell him not to be so stiff. Because he was still sweating, without asking, she brought him some napkins and a glass of ice water. Kevin took the water and drank it at once, and almost dropped the glass.

The whole while, Bertha was thinking, *What is wrong with this guy? He does not look like a criminal. He looks fairly decent. He is either clumsy or in love with my daughter or guilty of something. You never know these days.*

Kevin kept apologizing for dropping by without formally calling. Bertha again said, "Don't worry about a thing. She will be glad to see you."

"Are you sure?" asked Kevin, stuttering.

"Yes! Believe me, Mother knows. Mother always knows."

Kevin thought, *I am glad to hear that. This girl has given me little hint of encouragement. I wonder if she talks about me to her family.*

"So Kevin, I understand you came from the war? How was it?" asked Bertha.

"Ma'am, a war is a war; there is no fun in it. We just must do what we have to do."

"Do you think it was justified?"

"Ma'am, as soldiers, we just do what we are told to do. We do not question the merit of the war. We just obey orders. It is better like this. It keeps us focused on winning and overcoming the enemy. Soldiers play no politics. We're all Americans defending America at any cost."

"Were you ever scared?"

"Yes and no. We are usually scared of losing anyone in our ranks. But no one is scared of losing his life. Otherwise, we would not go out and fight. Every day is a brand new ball game. We can get blown away at any time. So, we go with one determination: get to the enemy first before he can get to us. Anytime we lose a companion, we feel like we have failed him and we want to make sure that no one dies in vain."

As Bertha was getting ready to ask some more questions, the front door swung open and Sophia walked in. Her eyes met Kevin's eyes. Bertha could feel the electricity. Kevin stood up.

"It's great to see you, Sophia! I am sorry to just show up like this, but I felt I had to come over to see how everyone was doing and if I could be of any help."

"Thanks for coming. Sorry you had to come at a time like this."

"That's ok. He is welcome here," Bertha interrupted.

"Of course! But I would have preferred to get the house back in order first."

"I am sorry Sophia. If you want I can leave, and I will see you another time," said Kevin, as he glanced to Sophia then to Bertha, who cut in again and said: "Don't be silly, you're already here! We welcome you." Then she softened and lowered her voice as if to whisper: "By the way, if you would excuse me, I need to say a few words to Sophia."

"By all means, please do."

Sophia and her mother went outside for a quick talk.

"What's the matter with you, Sophia? You are old enough to be more stable in that domain. Every time someone is interested in you, you seem to panic and give him the wrong message and make him run."

"What did I say, Mom?" Sophia said.

"Don't 'Mom' me. I am not finished yet. You need to start showing some interest in those who are interested in you. There are a lot of fish in the sea nowadays—"

"Mother!"

"I need you to get a life, get married, have children, and enjoy life."

"So you want me out of your house? Why didn't you just say so? Those days—when you needed to put your life on hold until someone came along to make you a somebody—are over, mother! I am everything I want to be just as I am. I do not need a man to give me worth or to make me enjoy life. I am doing fine. Besides, if people do decide to get married nowadays they usually wait until their thirties. They need time for education, a career, and financial stability before they commit themselves. What is the big deal about getting married anyway? People get divorced, it seems, a few days later—before they even finish paying the debt accrued for their wedding! I don't need this now."

"Of course honey, but things can be better. We'll talk later. Don't let the gentleman wait alone. He may leave!"

"Mother! In this day and age, people do not retain a partner. It is not the way it used to be in your time. In this century, you must play it tough to get rid of the unworthy. By the way, haven't you noticed the race difference? Are we that desperate?"

"Do as I say for now. Be courteous to everyone. No one knows the way things will turn out in life. Love crosses all boundaries."

Bertha and Sophia returned to the living room. Bertha excused herself and left Sophia and Kevin alone. Kevin felt she had become a bit more receptive than before, and wondering what her mother might have told her.

"Well Sophia, how is your father?"

"He is okay. As a matter of fact, let me see if he is ready to see visitors, and I will take you to see him."

She left the room and then came back quickly. "He is ready. Let's go."

Both of them went upstairs and saw Mr. Bernard Marcel who was sitting comfortably in a La-Z-Boy chair. They exchanged greetings and talked about general things for a few minutes. Then Kevin and Sophia returned downstairs. Kevin was dying to tell her how he felt. But he also knew that the time was not appropriate. After a short but cordial conversation, exchanging a few pleasantries, and setting up a make-up date with Sophia, Kevin did not want to press his luck, so he quit while he was ahead, with a brand new hope in his heart.

Saturday night was surprisingly nice. It felt like one of those late spring days. The weather was moderately warm, the birds were singing as they flitted through the trees under a cloudless turquoise sky. Before Sophia left the house, her mother decided to have a talk with her.

Mothers can be so caring and so loving that they may become irrational sometimes. Bertha wanted to make sure that her daughter was properly dressed and that the colors matched, and that there was not too much cleavage showing. She wanted to be reassured that Sophia smelled good but with a subtle perfume; she inspected the nails, the shoes, everything. She even offered to drive her there. Sophia had to put her foot down and tell her, "NO!" So Bertha gave her a $100 bill, just in case she needed to run away from him in a hurry and take a cab, even though Sophia had her car.

"What are you going to do tonight?" Bertha asked.

"Excuse me! Mom, when are you going to let go of me? I am an adult. I vote. I can handle myself."

Bertha replied, "I know you can, but can he? Can he resist seeing a gorgeous young lady without becoming an animal? Look at you, darling, don't you know you look like your mother. Even at my age, I can still stop traffic while crossing the street."

Sophia laughed, "I need to tell Dad about this. Mom, Kevin and I will be fine."

Bertha replied, "Speak for yourself, honey. Spare me that Kevin and I stuff."

"Mom, are you OK? One moment you want me out to go to get a life, and the next minute you treat me worse than a toddler!"

Bertha got by her and gently pinched her cheek while stating, "Only a mother can understand those mixed feelings. I don't want my baby to get hurt."

"Okay, Mom, relax. Everything is going to be fine."

"Let me tell you about dating—"

"Since when you have become an expert on dating, Mom?"

"How many types of dating do you know?"

"I don't know what on earth you are talking about, Mom!"

"Well, let me tell you quickly. There are two types: one is passive, where you are spectators, such as going to movies and shows; the other one is active, where you are an actor participating in the activities such as playing racquetball, cooking meals together—"

"Mom, you are really funny. You expect me and Kevin to go cook a meal? I don't believe that meal would be food—"

"Sophia!"

"I am only kidding, Mom" replied Sophia.

Bertha continued "Be careful where he takes you. You need to go to a decent place where you can stand or sit (but always with your feet on the ground) and talk like two civilized people and learn a thing or two about each other."

"Would you like to give me the topic, too?" asked Sophia, while she jingled some change in her hands.

"You can make fun of me, but I know what I am talking about. I have no objections to a respectable restaurant, a general audience movie where there is plenty of light, walking in well lit areas, or going to an art gallery or a decent concert." She paused a second then added, "My daughter does not go to cheap restaurants, or X-rated movies. She does not go dancing in questionable places, does not get into fast cars unless she is the driver. She does not go to rock concerts, or to any friends' houses. Just say No! Furthermore you do not take any drink he prepares for you. You ask for a soda, preferably a can that you can open yourself."

"Mother, you are out of your mind! What is so bad about rock concerts?"

Bertha replied, "My dear I have heard a lot about what happens in those concerts."

The phone rang, and Sophia automatically picked it up like a defeated boxer welcoming the sound of the bell ringing. She spoke in a low, sweet voice while her mother looked on. She hung up, and before Bertha could say one more word Sophia blurted out: "It was Kevin. He wanted to know if he should pick me up. I said no."

Bertha replied "Very good!" and then she called her husband: "Bernard, Bernard, Bernard!" she cried out at the top of her lungs. Bernard was standing right behind her as she bellowed.

"What is it that you need Bertha?" asked Bernard calmly.

"Go and take Sophia to her date."

"Honey, last time I checked, Sophia had a car and she knew how to drive."

"Thank you, Dad! How do I look?"

Bernard replied, "Fantastic! Now go out and break a leg."

Bertha put her hands on her head and said with disbelief, "What?"

Sophia jumped, kissed them both and left.

This time Sophia was there way before Kevin.

When he saw her, it was like greeting sunshine in the evening. He was in awe of her beauty. She wore a simple but elegant outfit, a scarf, a streamlined pencil skirt, and a V-neck blouse. She looked dazzling. She gazed at her surroundings while his mouth dropped. He gave her a smile as big as Mount Everest. Sophia was elegant, and amazingly beautiful. They sat outside; the musicians were playing blues. He felt as if she was so beautiful he could not give her a full gaze at once. From time to time he glanced at her, like a cat prowling around the milk-jug, knowing full well the master may be watching him. Finally, Kevin tried to start talking to Sophia about his feelings. Strangely enough, to his dismay, it was as if he were becoming mute. The words would not come out. Unexpectedly, Sophia almost fell off her chair; he jumped to her rescue and spontaneously asked her: "Are you ok, dear?" Before he waited for the answer, he realized he could talk after all, so he began:

> "Sophia, I have told you this already—when I was a boy, in elementary school, I used to think about you all the time. I even drew your picture and hung it by my bed. My sister used to tease me. I could never tell you. You were so bright and so articulate; you were very intimidating. I was afraid of you. Consequently, I kept it a secret. No. The truth is I told a few guys. They agreed with me that you wouldn't accept me. One

of our teachers even told me it was just a crush, and I would get over it."

Sophia interrupted him and asked him in a teasing tone, "Are you still afraid of me?" Then, without giving his answer, Kevin continued by saying in a soft voice:

"When my parents had to move, it was a hard blow. I had to leave the beautiful house where we lived. I had to leave my friends, some of whom I would never see again; worst of all, I knew I was going to be away from you. Unfortunately, youngsters have no say in those decisions. No adults really weigh our concerns seriously. We are there to listen and obey. Wherever the parents go, we can only pack up and follow. Nevertheless, my siblings and I, we left with heavy hearts. There are a few people I never forgot, especially you. Believe me; I could not forget you, even though I must admit I tried. After a few semesters in college, I enlisted in the army. I did the rest, if not most, of my equivalent collegiate studies while in the military. I went to war. I escaped death many times. However, thank heaven, I am still alive. I became involved with a few girls in the past here and there, but you lingered in my mind. I wanted to let you know how I feel about you."

"Tell me something, how many girls have you had?" asked Sophia in an amused tone.

With half a smile, Kevin shrugged his shoulders as if to say *I am not sure.*

"So they were so many, you are not sure?"

"None, I am not the father of any girls. I have no children," Kevin replied sarcastically.

"Don't play dumb with me! How many girls have you gotten involved with? How did you find my phone number and address, Kevin?"

Kevin chose to ignore the first question and to the second one:

"Finding you was nerve-racking. I knew your first name was Sophia, and I knew you were either Marcel or Joseph. But I was thinking of your buddy who was always with you—Lakisha. I kept asking: which one was it? Was it Lakisha Joseph and Sophia Marcel or was it Lakisha Marcel and Sophia Joseph? The dilemma was, there are many Josephs in the phone book, and I did not know your address."

"So how long did it take you to come up with my number?" asked Sophia intrigued.

"To make a long story short: I had to go to several libraries, to the old school district, then to the school itself. After several screenings and authorizations, I finally got our old school records. Thank God your parents never changed their phone number, even though you guys might have moved."

"I am impressed. Why did you go through so much trouble?"

"Isn't it obvious? Imagine you had the opportunity to get to a precious treasure, and you knew it was rare and difficult to get but you knew your life depended on it; would you hesitate to go through any challenge to get to it?"

"What makes you think the treasure is not a lready taken?"

"It's a chance I had to take. Is it taken?"

Sophia deflected the question. She thought about the few guys who had approached her; somehow she felt Kevin was different. He sounded sincere. Despite all resistance, she felt she was falling for him big time. Something about him made her fall head over heels in love with him, yet she needed to be sure and decided to continue to play hard to get. She asked the following question:

"What do you want from me Kevin? I am not sure I understand the point or the purpose of all these back and forth conversations, meetings, etc."

"Excuse me for beating around the bush. I told you I was not too good at expressing myself. What makes the situation so difficult… I only know three words to express myself. Words you have heard many times before. They are simple, have even become lame, cliché. But out of an overwhelming feeling, I want you to know, Sophia, that I LOVE YOU! I want you to know that ever since I met you years ago I was in love with you. But, they always say that kids know nothing about love. They even talk about infa—infatua—"

As Kevin was stuttering, Sophia filled in. "You mean infatuation!"

Kevin replied: "Yes! Infatuation. After all those years apart, I've had the chance to learn more about life. I have had more than a few very unpleasant experiences, especially in war. I have become more mature. I am here to tell you, all that time my life was on hold. My heart is beating at the rhythm of your desires. It is like a safe and you are the only one with the combination. You are the sparkle of my life."

"You like metaphors, don't you? Maybe I lost the combination. How can you be sure it is not infatuation?"

"Sophia, you and I know that infatuation is a short-lived, overwhelming intense attraction; it is passion. It is baseless and blurs all judgment. But for me it is totally different. I want you to know that I love you. Everyday that passes by, my love for you never ceases to grow stronger. Would you give me the chance to show that love. Would you give me the opportunity to share that love with you? I have come to that stage in life when I need a long-term partner for my life. Would you seriously consider my request?"

"I am very flattered Kevin. But this is coming out of nowhere and so quickly. I need to think about it all."

"I understand. But don't think too hard and don't take too long. My heart is on life support right now."

While the musicians played *Take a Chance on Me*, Kevin and Sophia seemed to be enjoying each other's company. Both ate very little of what they ordered while exchanging sweet nothings here and there. But most of the dialogue occurred by telepathy. Unfortunately, they had no power over time. The clock kept its inexorable ticking and it was getting late. Kevin escorted Sophia to her car. She thanked him for a nice evening. This time he kissed her on her cheek and they said goodbye to each other. She sped away while Kevin was left standing still, his arms crossed over his chest as if to support his heart in a sling, looking on as she disappeared into the horizon.

When she was sure she was out of his sight she slowed down. Before going home, she went for a slow drive by the beach. She opened the sunroof and all the windows to let some air in; she felt as if she were going to suffocate. There was hardly a soul around because by that time in the season it was a bit chilly. She felt as if a heavy burden had been placed on her shoulders. She stopped for a while. She looked up without seeing the sparkle of the clouds. *What is it about this man that is different from the others? I need to figure that out. After Billy, Joshua, Bryan and others, I was convinced that men were a bunch of vultures seeking to destroy their prey in order to devour their flesh. These days, most of them use all the tricks in the book just to get what they want. They know what tune to play to impress you, to catch you off guard, and to zap you before you know it. There are a bunch of players who use the word love to satisfy their own selfish desires. What is love anyway? I was told it was a sincere sentiment to communicate one's feelings and to do your best to make the other happy. But somehow I seem to attract a bunch of trash. Deep inside, after Bryan, I decided to stay away from men and to go on with my life. I promised myself to run as fast as I could away from their grip. I have excellent parents who have always supported me—although at times they are too pushy and too loving—but I can live with that. I have plans to pursue further studies, to continue to work and gain experience in a law firm while enjoying a great single life. Free as a bird! I was looking forward to traveling as I please, working in a field that I like, helping the poor and the sick, vacationing here and there—what a great life: to be able to go through it care free, at my own pace, not having to adjust. Love can be so inconvenient. It forces you to care, to worry, to be hurt, to be uncomfortable, and to compromise. For me love is nothing but a blister, a thorn to bleed my flesh. I could do without it. Yet I love the way it makes you feel. The ecstasy, the passion it arises. Then it again breaks your heart. How happy I was leading my own little personal life, carefree, with no one to accommodate, to inquire about. But, suddenly, out of nowhere, Kevin had to burst into my life and I feel helpless, restless, and breathless. This brings me another wave of a different happiness. I feel elated, important, worthy of any man's love. I feel as if I am going to concede, although I know I may get hurt. I thought I had all the doors and windows closed. I put up a big sign everywhere: I AM DONE WITH LOVE. But love is shameless. What a weed! Here it comes again and it is overpowering me. I don't know what to do. I feel it is going to win again. That's not fair. Please go away, love! Let me live in peace! I do not need this kind of love, not now, not ever! But my heart is already melting. Why? Why now, why him, why me? My ego says NO to any man, but my heart says YES to Kevin. I want all men to suffer, to be punished and to be cursed for their wickedness, their lies, their attitude, their arrogance. They do not care about anyone but themselves. They have no conscience. They want a girl for each season; worse yet, they think we are disposable like that bottle of cognac they throw away after drinking the contents. Somehow Kevin seems different, yet I know he wants the same things. I know he is another man, yet I feel his heart and mine are like two wings of the same love bird. I feel he is closer to me. But is he really? I know what he may do, yet if there must be one more to break my heart again, I think I want him to be the one? What do I do? What do I do, dear God? I am hopelessly attracted to him. I have no more strength to resist him. How much longer can I pretend?*

The radio was playing *For All We Know*, and as she continued to think and talk to herself, with tears spilling down her cheeks, her mother called her on her cell phone.

"Sophia, where are you? Kevin just called wanting to know if you got home safely."

"Don't worry mother, I am on my way." She hung up and hurried to get home.

Sophia made it there a few minutes before midnight. Mother was there waiting to hear all the details. Sophia did not even have the chance to use her key; Bertha opened the door, gave her a big hug, and started singing.

"Mother, what's the matter with you?"

"Don't play dumb with me. He told you he loves you, didn't he?"

"How do you know? Were you spying on us? Did Kevin tell you anything? Why are you so interested in him?

"I have a good feeling about him. Before he came over to our home, I felt something crawling in my right foot. That's a good sign."

"Come on Mom, you are pulling my leg now. What am I going to do with Bryan?"

"Bryan? You still keep contact with that fellow. I don't like him. He has no manners, no job, no future—"

"Mother, how do you know that? You always judge people by their appearance. That's wrong."

"Have you ever heard the saying that a tree is identified by its fruit? Someone who comes to my house on a motorcycle, with tattoos all over his body, exposing a pierced navel, earrings, and his pants down to his knees, sweating, attempting to kiss me and calling me Mom the first time he sees me is definitely not our type."

"Our type? What type are we? Tell me mother. Your type is suit and tie, Mercedes Benz, Wall Street—"

"That's enough Sophia! If there is one thing you must never forget, it is the fact that we raised you with values, ethics, and high expectations. We love you and we are always looking out for you. We do not want you to go through the bad experiences we have gone through. At my age, I can spot a loser a thousand miles away. We do not want you to be hurt. We do not want you to be stuck with someone you have to support all your life. Life is tough. Why not avoid an obvious disaster? Why play a martyr when you can avoid it?"

As tears ran down Bertha's cheeks, Sophia softened up her tone a little. She said, "But Mom, when you are young, in the struggle between the heart and the mind the heart usually wins. As young people, you dream of one magic moment, when you will meet that special someone that will strike you like lightning, sweep you off your feet, and transport you up above the clouds while your heart is quivering and you are giddy with desire. The brain may say no, but you go with the heart, even though you suspect you have made a bad move. You do not care. You will deal with it later. You were young once; is it too long to remember how it used to be?"

"No, my dear! I still remember being young and that is what is killing me inside—watching you."

"So, do you want to tell me about yourself in those days? For once, relax and tell me!"

"Not now Sophia. This is your moment. I do not want to rain on your parade. How was dinner?"

"You don't give up, do you?" Sophia replied, and then continued, pretending to ignore the urgent request: "Last time I saw Bryan, I told him to leave me alone. I would have let him go earlier, but you and Dad were so against him. I wanted to give him his fair chance. Finally, I decided to break up with him because we disagreed on almost everything. He was immature, he was too insecure, he was too pushy, he stressed me out, and he was unpredictable. He was rude, vulgar, and only wanted one thing. Sometimes I wondered if he had other girlfriends. He disappeared for days and would never talk about it. That guy was too mysterious for me. Two months ago he left after a big argument about nothing. Since then, I haven't heard from him. But strangely enough, sometimes I miss him. I think he needs me."

"No, I think he needs help. I mean professional help!"

"I did not know you were a psychologist, Mom."

"Listen, common sense, experience, following your gut instinct will tell you a lot. You just proved my point. Kevin just heard about the fire, and he came to visit. Where is that Bryan?"

"Mom, I do not want you to look down on my friends. For you guys, everything is so clear, so black and white: someone shows up well dressed in a brand new car, speaks nicely, lies through his teeth because he knows what to say to the girls and to their parents to gain their trust and you are ready to accept him and treat him like a prince. Things have changed. What I want in life is not what you have. Kevin is telling me he has always loved me; how do I know that? What do I know about him? How can I be sure?"

"Sophia my dear, listen to me." They both walked into Sophia's room and closed the door. "Let me review with you some basic principles about picking up a partner."

"I am not picking up a partner—" Sophia said.

Bertha interrupted Sophia and said, "Okay, whatever! Let me remind you about some basic facts of life in general: All of us want to be happy and successful in everything we do and in every aspect of our lives. Nevertheless, most of us fail to make it. How come? Let me tell you a little secret: Life hinges on two facts—who we are, and the nature of our relationship with our surroundings. The prerequisite for being successful is preparation, knowledge, and the application of what we have learned."

"Who are we?" Sophia teased.

"As you may know, Sophia, human beings are complicated and are the products of many factors.

"Didn't you and Dad go over all these with us before?" asked Sophia, a bit annoyed.

"It is worth reviewing," replied Bertha. "Despite common organs and features, each of us is unique. What is it that makes us tick? Here are four factors to take into consideration:

1. Genetics, heredity, how and where a person was born and how he or she grows up, the style and type of household, mother's and father's roles, trauma, stress, perception of the parents.

2. School, church, community, books, media, and friends.

3. The evolving society and current general views on types of relationships, the definition of family, and acceptance modalities.

4. The types of personality, character (jealous, unhappy, always complaining, hard to please, moody or unstable, flirtatious, superior, or infallible, on the negative side; or mature, patient, altruistic, disciplined, responsible, hard-working, communicative, positive, persevering, constructive, knowledgeable, committed, and willing to make marriage work, on the positive side.

All have their part to play.

So, if you want to settle down and have a lasting relationship, you must not take it lightly. You need to know if it is achievable. You must do your homework. Would you jump out of a moving plane without knowing how to use a parachute or without making sure the one you have works properly? Would you jump into a pool or the sea without knowing how to swim? Would you get behind the wheel without knowing how to drive? So why would you venture into a romantic relationship that can have a lasting impact on your destiny without the proper preparation?

Young people strongly believe that love means *'let it flow as it goes; whatever happens, happens; and we'll see how far it goes.'* I was young once. But as I got older I learned the hard way that you must be prepared to handle a relationship. Of course theoretical knowledge alone is not enough, but it sure can help make a difference.

What do you know about yourself? Your past can be a source of blessing as well as a curse in your quest toward a successful romantic life. The misconceptions and prejudices you were taught, the shortcomings you saw in others, your cultural conditioning, family traditions, your spiritual biases, your education, social upbringing, your tastes, habits, tendencies, gifts, and talents—these are the challenges to meet head on. Your personality, temperament and biases—are they still haunting you? You must find a way to overcome them; otherwise you will have a maladjustment situation.

By the time you are self-conscious enough to be interested in love, most of the myths and beliefs are already in you. The way you were raised and the experiences you went through make you who you are at this moment: shy, lonely, selfish, arrogant, and stubborn, a spoiled brat—or enthusiastic, respectful of others, friendly, conciliatory, eager to learn, and willing to compromise.

This is why raising children is such a challenging task. Whatever they learn will mark them for life. You already have your bad habits. Nevertheless, it is never too late. The main thing is the ever present willingness to learn and change for the better and not be bitter. It is said, *'If you don't love yourself, how can you love anybody else?'* The fact of the matter is, you cannot give what you do not have. If you love yourself without being selfish and narcissistic about it, if you have a generally good feeling about yourself; if you have confidence with a positive attitude, you will go out looking for the best. You will convey and project that great positive attitude and confidence. However, if you have a poor self-image, an inferiority complex, and are immature, you are likely to become jealous, irritable, possessive, isolated, even rude and violent. You said earlier you do not want what I have. That's fine; I do not think you are entirely sure of what you want. So, why not work with the model you have and alter it and adjust it as you go along. Do not reject it from the beginning, and start looking for something when you do not even know what it should look like. You run the risk of accepting an imitation or something far less than what you deserve. Believe me Sophia, you deserve the best. When you are young, bright, and beautiful, as you are, the world is at your feet. You can pick and choose. So I beg you, pick the best. I intend to help you do that."

"Even against my will?" Sophia asked in a teasing tone.

"Yes! So I can die in peace."

"Here we go again; you want me to feel guilty if I do not go along with your strange ideas."

"Sophia, ultimately, the choice is always yours. I won't be here forever. You know what? I always wondered that if young folks do not trust their parents, why not choose another trustworthy adult for advice?"

"Because we know we can make excellent choices too," Sophia protested.

"The best way to go about it is to get advice from experienced people, from different sources, and make your own decisions."

"You should have been a lawyer," Sophia said.

Both of them laughed so loud that Bernard yelled from the master bedroom: "Do you guys know what time it is? I need some rest to go to work in a few hours."

Bertha hugged her daughter and said: "To be continued," and then she left to go to sleep.

Sophia managed not to give a specific answer to Kevin's pressing question as to whether or not they could make plans for a long-term relationship. Nevertheless, they continued to see each other on a regular basis. Kevin used every excuse under the sun to see her, bring her gifts, cards or love notes, or send her text messages and email. They went to concerts, movies, the theater, the gym, boat and car shows, barbecues and picnics; they went canoeing, bicycling, bowling, and ice skating together. It was as if one was the shadow of the other.

Sophia's parents had never seen her so happy, and that also made them happy. One day Kevin came to see Sophia, but she was not there. Bertha believed in five basic principles in order to have a reliable impression about any young man:

1. Family background, faith, and values

2. Personal habits, self-esteem, self worth, self actualization, money management, and manners

3. Viewpoint about women

4. Viewpoint about life in general, and interactions with others

5. Personal goals in life

Bertha decided to test those basic principles on Kevin.

"So Kevin, we haven't heard much about your parents. What can you say about them?"

"Well, Mom told me she met Dad while he was in boot camp and she was doing some volunteer work there as an aspiring nurse. It was love at first sight. After graduation, they got married. Dad was the third generation to embrace military service. He loved it very much. I have one brother and one sister. Both are older and are enjoying their lives. My sister Ana works as a secretary and my brother is a handyman who has always had big dreams. When my dad died during a military maneuver in the Middle East, I was still in junior high school. Years before his death, he lost his left leg in combat. But he remained fairly stoic about it. He was active until that unfortunate fatal accident. Then my mom had to struggle with us as a widow, a single mother, so to speak. Dad did not leave much. She had a rough time. We, the children, did not make it easy for her at all. She was always a determined woman. I don't know where she got her strength. She is a tough act to follow. She is not one of those intellectuals, but she sure is full of common sense and knowledge. She never complained, and was never jealous of or rude to people. You should see her now! She is my hero. When she goes out with us, people believe she is our sister. She has such fond memories of my dad that when I finished high school I felt compelled to follow in his footsteps. After a year or so in college, I enrolled in the military myself. I just came back from combat in Iraq."

"So what do you plan to do now?" asked Bertha.

"I may go back for another two years—"

"Really!" interrupted Bertha a bit puzzled. She was

thinking to herself: Why come after my daughter when you want to go back for more military service? Do you plan to use her and then dump her to go away, leaving her at the mercy of circumstances?

Kevin seemed to realize he might have made a mistake, and he added quickly, "But I am not so sure. Time will tell."

"In case you don't go back, what else you have in mind to do?" asked Bertha.

"I have a couple of interviews for computer programming, lined up on Wall Street. My eyes are ultimately on owning my own business. In a few months, I should know for sure what I'm going to do. Right now I am helping my mother to settle down in a better neighborhood."

"So where do you see yourself five to ten years from now?"

"Wow! Frankly Mrs. Marcel, I am evaluating all my options in order to choose what is best for me, my future family, and my children. Such a decision is contingent upon who my life partner is. We need to discuss it together."

Bertha seemed pleased with that answer, so she moved right onto another topic.

"When you lived here before, what was your address?"

"I used to live around East Flatbush, by some dead end street, in a big old house there. We used to have mixed feelings about it, but I still remember my room."

"Why did you guys have mixed feelings?"

"We had mosquitoes in the summer and a constant cold draft in the winter. But it was always fun. We spent time together with friends."

"I understand that your last name is Constanzo."

"Yes! I am Kevin Constanzo."

"Constanzo!" She rolled up her eyes and paused. I knew a Constanzo family. They had a big store downtown where Bernard and I used to do most of our shopping. Are you related to them in any way? Mr. Constanzo had a blue Dodge and a big German Shepherd."

"That was my uncle! My mom worked there part-time, and my dad liked to work there when he was on leave from active duty. You probably met them once or twice too," replied Kevin with a broad smile.

"Yes! I think I remember your mom. She told me she had four children, but I never met them."

"Now you are looking at one of them." said Kevin. My brother is George junior, and my sister is Ana. The fourth one was my sister Maria, who died in a car accident years ago."

"I am sorry to hear that. So how is the rest of the family?"

"Fine! Everybody is fine."

"What a small world!" As Bertha was getting ready to press on with more questions, Sophia came home. Kevin was delighted to see her. Bertha said, "Give my regards to your mom, brother, and sister."

"I will!"

As Sophia came in, Bertha decided to leave before raising any suspicion from her daughter. She excused herself and left Kevin alone with Sophia.

Later on, Bertha came in to bring them something to drink. She caught them exchanging a passionate kiss.

They did not see her. She walked slowly and quietly backward and disappeared.

She went to see her husband, Bernard, who was always either reading, writing or paying bills. He hardly watched TV. This time he was reading one of Shakespeare's masterpieces. Once Bertha walked in, he acknowledged her presence, put down the book, removed his glasses, and stretched. Bernard said, in his usual eloquent voice, "Beloved, what's on your mind?"

"Nothing," replied Bertha, smiling.

"Did you bring me some good news?"

"Nothing is new, Bernard. Nothing!"

"Our daughter's mood seems to be more stable lately. She smiles, she laughs, she kids around, she sings, and she is back to her old self. This is something new Bertha, isn't it?"

"Oh yes! What a relief! For too many years this girl has been driving us crazy."

"You can say that again! Sophia had such an uneventful childhood. She was the brightest kid, always jovial, well mannered and eager to help. Remember how people always wanted to steal her away from us? Then came her teenage years and all hell broke loose. She became rebellious and rude, with poor impulse control; she was depressed, and had morbid thoughts. She has been really difficult to get along with. I wonder if something happened to her. But she will never tell us."

Bernard added, "The worst part is every time we see some improvement, we expect the progress to continue, and then she goes back and does worse than before. It seems her goal in life has been to find out what we want and to do exactly the opposite. Even now, no one really knows for sure what she is up to."

"What a stressful life for parents in this century!" exclaimed Bertha. "You do your best, based on what you know is right, then contrary to what you expect, you see a totally different result. Right under your eyes the kid is embarking on a road that is surely going to lead to some kind of trouble. Then you start to feel guilty. You ask yourself: where did I go wrong? What can I change? What did I do to generate so much hostility, so much hatred from someone I love so much? It is a serious war where both parties risk losing. Heaven knows, we have been through hell."

Bernard interrupted, "We still have reasons to be grateful. We never gave up. We continued and will continue to love them. They are still alive. And there is always hope when there is life. So many parents have lost their kids either through drugs, accidents, or gunshot wounds; others are in jails here and there; and others do not do anything except wander around.

The other day I was talking to a colleague of mine. He told me how his only son, who is twenty-three years old, in law school, could not continue because he became psychotic. He has watched his bright young man who made him so proud slowly deteriorate and go downhill, with limited results even with medications, fighting with him almost daily to take his meds, begging the hospitals to admit him for his own safety, fighting against the system and the established rules that cannot admit someone against his will unless he actually does something harmful to himself or others. He told me—with tears in his eyes—that if he had a choice he would rather see his son dead of a physical illness. He would have buried him, mourned him, and had closure after such a loss. But with his condition, he sees him dying slowly and daily, while living a life that is killing the father himself. All over the world, so many parents are crying because their children are in jail, others are addicted to drugs or are involved in illicit acts, and teenagers are pregnant or have sexually transmitted diseases or even incurable infections. Only parents know what parents go through. So, overall, we can be thankful, Bertha. Our children are okay."

Bertha added, "Maybe there should be an international parents anonymous club where all of us can share our grief and our pleasure. Today's kids can be spoiled by bad influences even though they stay home. Between the Internet and television, they usually choose the worst of both worlds." On a more determined note she said, "Overall we can say we are blessed. Junior didn't go to college, but he is working and on his own. Although he did not follow in his father's footsteps—a secret dream of most parents with prestigious jobs—he is doing well. And Sophia seems to be looking forward to law school."

Bernard added, "What is the story between her and that guy Kevin? Is this going anywhere, or is it another period of foolishness?"

Bertha chose not to answer that question. Instead, she hugged her husband, and hand in hand, they took a few steps toward the window looking down as Kevin and Sophia walked slowly in the yard toward Kevin's car. There was a full moon in a clear starry sky. Some migrating creatures were flying happily. Once Kevin said goodbye to Sophia, Bernard and Bertha also decided to hit the sack.

8

Friday night was usually a special occasion for the family. Everyone gathered around the table. They talked about the significant events of the week, they read, they sang, they prayed, and they laughed. This Friday evening was particularly special: it snowed all day. The roads were mostly covered, and there were heavy winds; everything conspired to make it a homebound night. Dad came in and expected the usual. However, Sophia was not there to play the piano. Bertha said that Sophia went to do her hair. So the rest of the family gathered as usual. Dad was obviously disappointed, even upset. How could Sophia dare ignore the family tradition that she grew up with? The only happy camper was Junior, because he knew that when his turn came, he could always refer to Sophia's absence to excuse himself in the future.

After supper, everyone retreated to their personal activities. Junior was in the basement, talking business with someone on his cell phone. Bertha and Bernard remained in the living room catching up on some reading and commenting on some news with some on and off napping in between. Then along came Sophia, way past 11 PM.

"Hi Mom, hi Dad!" She embraced them as if she was just going through the motions, and then flew into her room. This was so strange that Bertha and Bernard decided to follow her. They knocked and joined her.

Bernard always looked serious. You could never know what was going on inside him. Every now and then he would explode when he felt that things were getting to be too much or when he wanted to warn against imminent danger. Usually, he saw the children along with his wife Bertha, when some disciplinary measures were needed.

Furthermore, anytime he said 'Mademoiselle Sophia' or 'Mr. Junior' or 'Madam Bertha', you knew something was definitely wrong.

Bernard came in and sat down on Sophia's bed; Bertha sat in Sophia's chair by the window. That in itself was strange. Usually, it was the other way around. Bertha's eyes were avoiding Sophia's. Bernard started clearing his throat and began with "Mademoiselle Sophia" and Sophia knew she must be in trouble.

> "Yes Dad, I am sorry for missing our family gathering. I know how much it means to you. But honestly, I lost all track of time."
>
> "Do you remember how important it is for this family to have weekly meetings?" Dad asked.
>
> "Yes I do!"
>
> "Well, you missed it, so your mother and I feel like having one now. This is your unique session in the comfort of your room."
>
> Sophia stated: "Now? Why? Where is Junior? What's wrong? Can I have a rain check?"
>
> "Calm down. Nothing is wrong. We just want to talk," interjected Bertha.
>
> "I have a lot on my mind now. This is not the best time," sobbed Sophia.
>
> "No time is the best time. With my schedule, yours,

Junior's, and your mother's, we are lucky to remember what each other looks like," said Bernard.

"If you insist on talking, then go ahead. I don't promise you I will be too engaging now."

Bernard began in a grave voice "First of all, your mother and I must acknowledge the significant improvement in your demeanor. You have become more outgoing and joyful. You seem to have a steady relationship with that gentleman of yours. We do not believe it is too much to ask that you let us know what you two plan to do together. As you know, we are sociable beings. Any time two people are seeing each other on a steady basis, there must be some clear understandings as to how far the two want to go. Otherwise, one of them is going to be hurt and disappointed. So it is not far-fetched to determine a few things:

1. Why are you together? Is it because you want to have fun together while you can and change as the days go by? To show friends you can have significant relationship too, or to get out away from home? To have a better financial condition and share the bills? Or is it because of commitment, love? Then what do you mean by love? How can you be sure is it not just lust?

2. Do you have the capacity to take inventory of yourself? Are you mature enough to show love and realize that it grows slowly and should get stronger with time? True love is not possessive, but respects and allows the partner enough room to grow. Are you willing to seek advice and guidance?

3. What do you know about the urge and the role of sexual intimacy?

4. What can you bring into the relationship?

5. What is the profile of an eventual partner? What do you know about his or her family upbringing, types of discipline, role of mother and father, closeness to family traditions and current relationship with parents, types of parents, types of childhood, values, personalities, education, and beliefs about various subjects including those considered as taboo or inappropriate by certain people.

6. Are you able to see you in the real fashion? Reality check: Can you admit you are not perfect? Are you willing to take the necessary steps to improve yourself or do you blame everybody else or the circumstances or the environment for all your shortcomings? No one is perfect. The key is to have the determination to be the best you can be and not to give up when the old you shows up unexpectedly and embarrasses you. Be on your guard, and do your best in good faith. No one can require more than that.

Your mother and I believe you and Kevin have been seeing each other long enough to want to know whether or not the two of you are going somewhere or just wasting each other's time. The worst thing that can happen is to keep going when you have seen so many obvious signs to call it quits and linger around hoping for a miracle."

"What are you guys talking about?" Sophia interrupted. "Are you saying we should start sending out invitations for our wedding? You guys always come up with #1, 2, 3, 4, and 10. Real life does not go like this."

"Tell me about it," responded Bertha.

"Mom, Dad, the old generation has a lot of myths and legends about marriage—"

"Yes," replied Bernard, "and here are a few:

Myth #1 Marriage is the solution to all affection problems.

Answer: No. It can solve some and can complicate others. It all depends on the given situation. For example, if two people really love each other and are willing to make a long-lasting commitment, the answer is yes. Your mother and I are a good example. But if people are getting married just to have sex or just to join the incomes to pay bills, they are likely to be disappointed.

Myth #2 Marriage is for everyone.

Answer: Again the answer is no. Some people are not marriage material—not marriageable—and they will never be. Only their mother or their father can put up with all their weaknesses and their excuses.

Myth #3 Marriage makes you a complete being.

Answer: Wrong. You do not need to get married to be propelled into a complete being.

Myth #4 Marriage will change the partners for the better.

Answer: Do not bet on it. There may be some improvement, but most of the time, the flaws you see during courtship may even be worst after, when the partners may reveal their true selves.

Myth #5 In marriage, you are partners in a fifty-fifty contribution.

Answer: In marriage, everyone must do the maximum, regardless of what the other partner may bring. Your contribution should not depend on the other partner. It is a selfless commitment, with dedication toward the other partner.

Myth #6 Love is reciprocal; once in love always in love.

Answer: Love wants to germinate and blossom. However, human beings only look out for themselves. If things keep going against them, sooner or later there will be consequences.

Myth #7 True love immunizes against infidelity.

Answer: True love will definitely play a key role in faithfulness. However, other measures must be taken to prevent people from succumbing to temptation.

Myth #8 People in love always get along.

Answer: This is not always true. A balanced relationship, based on mutual respect, freedom to choose and sound judgment will allow disagreement without being disagreeable."

Bertha added quickly, "Obviously, for the new generation, the myths about marriages mean you can be happy, have a good time, and live a fulfilled life alone or with any partner for as long as you see fit. This revolutionary idea is not going to convince me. Moral values and history are on our side. As a matter of fact, the more we change things to satisfy the new generation, the more likely things will get worse. The politicians don't have the guts to put their feet down and say *'enough is enough.'* So everyone is going down the wrong path until we reach the end of our rope and head into our own extinction. Our role here is to guide you. We are talking about you, our daughter, and we want the best for you."

"Dad, how do you know that someone is marriage material?

"Excellent question," responded Bernard. "It depends. A man is "marriage material" when he knows what a woman wants in any long lasting relationship."

"What does a woman want?" asked Sophia.

"You should know," replied Bernard, smiling.

"Well, I can point out a few things," interrupted Bertha. "A woman wants to be treated like the only queen in the man's life. This means getting respect, being appreciated and well cared for financially and romantically, being remembered on special occasions, and being listened to."

Sophia added, "There is not much difference between then and now. I want my man to be good looking, fit, well mannered, affectionate, a great lover, able to tell a few jokes here and there, able to play different roles in different levels of society without embarrassing me, a responsible provider with enough time for me when I need him, sensible enough to surprise me now and then with thoughtful gifts and actions, able to listen, communicate and carry a decent conversation. I need a man who cares!"

"It is not going to be easy, Sophia," said Bertha, while looking at Bernard out of the corner of her eyes to see his facial expression.

Bernard took over and said: "Now it is my turn to tell you what a man really would like from a woman.

"I want—"

"Let us not get too personal. Let's talk in general," interrupted Bertha.

"Okay," replied Bernard, who instinctively pulled up his sleeves as if to give the fight of his life. He felt he was mandated to talk on behalf of all men. It looked like he had been waiting for this moment all his life. After thirty-five years of marriage, he obviously knew a thing or two about what a man needed.

"Well, a man wants an honest and intelligent lady who remains attractive and elegant, who helps to keep the house clean and peaceful with the least amount of junk possible. She must not whine and nag. She is someone who is relaxed, a partner who is diligent, shares his prowess and encourages him through his shortcomings, and is not a permanent competitor destroying him through negative comments, looking down on him and comparing him with all her friends' husbands. She must inspire confidence, faithfulness, and pride in society. She must be willing to give him space to breathe, tell him what she wants and not play the guessing game. She needs to be genuinely interested in his leisure time and activities, before and also after the marriage. When they go on vacation—"

"Hold it Dad. Vacation?"

"Hey, the last time I checked I had the floor," replied Dad, while Bertha crossed her arms in dismay and Sophia in amusement.

He went on: "As I was saying, when they go on vacation—"

Sophia interrupted again, "Why not save this part for later?"

"As you wish! Any place, any time, I am ready."

"But Dad, what about sex? You did not even mention that."

"Well, I believe, if it is done properly, wholeheartedly, with passion, romance and tenderness, a man and woman can both love sex. Of course there are instances due to the woman's cycle, malaise, illnesses, and hormonal changes, when it is less desirable. The man only needs to realize that affection, kindness, and caring do not necessarily mean sex. There is a time for everything. But believe me, although a normal man can think or look to be ready, there are circumstances when he may go through the motions and not be truly sexually active. It is like eating because there is plenty of food. But a real meal deserves the proper setting, time, and service, if you know what I mean."

It took Bertha and Bernard a while to realize that Sophia was already snoring while they were going at it with great fervor. So they quietly exited the room.

Kevin woke up early on Sunday morning. He seemed preoccupied with the status of his relationship with Sophia. He considered Sophia to be his elementary school sweetheart. He thought of her beautiful smile, her alto voice, her intelligence, her personality, and even the way that she walked. It all made her irresistible. Soon it would be one year since they had been going steady. Their love was blossoming. They saw each other regularly. They had begun to weigh in on each other's values, common interests, parents, childhoods, future plans, and beliefs. They had shared so many special occasions. Kevin wanted to move a step further because their ten months and two weeks together had been like heaven for him. He believed somehow Sophia felt the same way. His only concern was that she was too conservative, a bit too bossy, and too old fashioned and too close to her mother. But in the long run, this could work to his advantage.

Kevin's mother lived almost 1,700 miles away. He had not seen her for a while. He talked to her mostly about Sophia. So far, he had managed to not show Sophia's picture to his mother. She was intrigued. Kevin called his mother and told her that the following weekend he planned on to taking a few days off from his job at the Army recruiting station to drive all the way to Florida. Three days before his departure, the trip was canceled because of an impending hurricane. When Kevin called his mother, Nicole, to tell her the bad news, she did not sound too disappointed.

A few days later, while Sophia was busy studying, on Thursday evening, Kevin got home a bit early. So he decided to catch up and watch a few rented movies. He stayed up until one o'clock in the morning, and then he went to bed. Two hours later, someone was knocking at the door. Kevin got up and went to open the door. There stood his mother.

"Mother! What a pleasant surprise!"

"You know what they say: *'If Mohammed does not come to the mountain, the mountain must come to Mohammed,'*" replied his mother. "How is my baby doing? You look good, my son!"

"Mother, I can't tell you how happy I am to see you. What's new? Make yourself comfortable. Why didn't you call? I could have picked you up at the airport."

"Then, what would have happened to the surprise?" asked his mother.

"You look great, mother. I hope you are going to stay for a while; you and I have a lot of catching up to do."

"I plan to stay for a few days. We'll see. My reservation is for one week."

"I am glad to see you. You look great! What's new with you?" replied Kevin, who quickly managed to get things under control. They reminisced most of the night, and his mother chose to sleep on the sofa in the living room, so as to not trigger much disruption.

The following morning, Kevin left early while his mother was still sleeping. From his job, Kevin called his mother in the morning for some cordial talk. Nicole cleaned the place up and cooked. She also managed to go through the accessible things in the house, including several albums with a lot of pictures. Once Kevin got his major obligations taken care of, he rushed home to keep his mother company. Upon arriving, Kevin was in a good mood and was ready to engage in a meaningful conversation.

"How are you mother?"

Nicole replied with a cold, monotonic, disappointed voice, "I AM OKAY."

"What's wrong mother? You look different. Last night you were joyful, vigorous, and ready to go. What has happened today? Has anyone called? Are you all right? Do you have bad news?"

"Nothing is wrong," answered his mother.

"How is the rest of the family, mother?"

"Everyone is doing fine. Your sister gave birth to two beautiful babies: Sarah and Torah. The family is okay. Everybody is okay, except for me."

"You? What's wrong with you, mother?"

"Nothing! Life goes on!"

Although Nicole's sudden mood swing was—to say the least—bizarre, Kevin thought nothing of it. He enjoyed his mother's cooking, and expressed his gratitude. Nicole remained quiet but every now and then released a deep sigh. As he was getting up from the table, Nicole said to him:

"Kevin, I notice many pictures of you with a girl—"

Kevin interrupted with great excitement, "That girl is

Sophia. Isn't she beautiful? She is adorable! I can't wait for you to meet her—"

Nicole replied with a lukewarm attitude, "Is she the girl that you talk so much about every time we speak?"

"Yes!" replied Kevin.

Nicole's face dropped. After a long pause, and a few more sighs, she replied: "I hope you are not serious about this girl."

"Why not? You always told me to find the love of my life and settle down. Mother, she is the one!"

"But Kevin, she is different!"

"Really, how?" replied Kevin.

"Listen son, this is not a joke. I had no idea that girl you were so in love with was that kind."

"That kind? Wait a minute mother, what kind is that?"

"You know very well what I mean."

"No, seriously, from what you taught me, I do not know what you mean. Do you remember, as a kid, I once had a fight with another boy? I told you 'that N' boy beats me up. You told me to never speak that way about others. You went so far as to say—and I quote—'There is only one race: the human race; there is only one kind: mankind.'"

"Well, among all the things I taught you, you failed to remember all the other teachings but this one, didn't you?"

"I remember it because it opened my eyes. It has allowed me not to see people as black, white, yellow… but as human beings, God's creatures. Believe me, that sentence has relieved me from so many burdens. It has kept me humble, engaging, positive, and enthusiastic about life. By the way, you also told me that mankind is like a field of flowers. God made them in different colors, shapes, and forms to prevent life from being boring."

"I am happy you feel that way," replied Nicole. "But if my memory serves me correctly, I also taught you that you must measure every consequence of your action. People should live according to the accepted norms imposed by the society. Don't you know that our race is in peril? Soon, we will be the minority. Do you realize what this is? Do you care about what your children will look like? Maybe by then, most kids will be named Barak, anyway."

"What does that mean, mother? I am shocked. I am beginning to see a side of you I never knew before. All that time, I admired you as a hero. But now I see you are like those hypocrites who talk in public about fairness, equal rights, equal opportunities…but in private, deep inside you are full of bigotry, ignorance, prejudice, and arrogance."

"Maybe you should look at yourself too. You are selfish, inconsiderate, and insensitive. You don't know anything about interracial relationships, do you?"

"Tell me about it, mother. I'd love to hear your opinion."

"First of all, you are viewed as strange from both sides. The white folks would think you are maladjusted, an outcast, and unstable, someone with some kind of complex who has been rejected by the women in your race. The black side will see you as an outsider who is taking advantage of a naïve girl to compensate for some personal weaknesses, one who ignores history and wants to mess up his kids who, when born out of such a controversial union, won't know whether or not they are blacks, half-bred, cross bred, or white. You won't know what culture to teach your children."

"Mother, I appreciate your concern. Sincerely, your points are well taken."

"But I am not finished yet—"

"Well I already have an idea of what you are going to say. It's in that same frame of mind. I've heard it all from my friends—"

"I still need to finish: friends, you have to make new ones. Don't you realize that marriage has enough stress on its own without adding more pain and suffering? You will have to deal with people's reactions, stereotyped remarks, and looks; you will have to know where to travel with that lady—"

"Do you realize that we are living in the twenty-first century, the era where the world is one big village with all kinds of people? Don't you realize that even in the White House the barrier has fallen? Wake up mother. All you people seem to forget, I am Kevin. She is Sophia. All we care about is that we love each other. Do you remember how often you used to tell me how much you missed Dad, that many men have come after you, but you will never pay anyone of them any mind because no one can make you feel the way you felt with Dad? That no one could step into his shoes? Mother, I believe Sophia and I feel the same way about each other. The only problem is people like you, and your society that cares about us having different skin colors. You know what? Everyone can go to hell! Now I feel more strongly about Sophia than before."

"Love!" Nicole laughed. "It does not last forever like you hear in the songs, read in the novels, or see in the movies. Are you sure she feels the same way, Kevin? How do you know she is not using you to get even with some black guy who broke her heart before?"

"There you go again, stereotyping people. All of us can break someone's heart. This is not a racial issue. Haven't you read in the Bible that *man's heart is desperately wicked*? This is not unique to one group of people. The Europeans do it, Americans do it, and Caribbean people do it."

"I came all the way from Florida to spend some good time with my baby son. Instead, I get the shock of my life. I don't feel good. My heart is weak. My heart is hurting."

Nicole began to perspire heavily as she slumped into the sofa. EMS was called but by the time they came to take her to the hospital, she felt fine. She refused to go to the hospital. Kevin wondered: Could it be she was using a scare tactic? She used to be very manipulative. At any rate, Kevin decided to play it cool. He took her for a ride around the city. She did not want to go anywhere specific. They got back home and were about to go to bed, when the phone rang. Nicole picked it up. Sophia was on the other end:

"Yes, hello, this is Sophia. May I speak to Kevin, please?"

Nicole handed the phone to Kevin, who went to his bedroom for some privacy. She could not help overhearing Kevin saying, "That was your future mother-in-law who paid me a surprise visit. You will have time to meet her because she is not leaving anytime soon…"

When Kevin came out after the long phone conversation, his mother pretended to be sleeping. He left her alone and went back to bed.

Again the following morning, Kevin left early while Nicole was still in bed. When he came back home, the house was spotless but empty. His mother left him a note:

> *I want to remind you, Kevin, the choosing of a soulmate is not done haphazardly. You need to take into consideration:*
>
> *1. The whole person: physical appearances, and mental and intellectual capacities*
> *2. The family background*
> *3. Moral values and religious beliefs*
> *4. The financial potential*
> *5. Role in the society and its reaction*
> *6. The potential for future growth in terms of both growing old together and of your progeny.*
>
> *By the way, as I told you, Ana just had two babies. She has her hands full. So I decided to go to see her. I am sure she can definitely use my help without breaking my heart.*
>
> *Love, Mother*

Kevin became so furious that he lost control and punched a hole in the kitchen wall with his right fist. He went out, took a walk, and stepped into a movie theater. Then, feeling bored, he returned home and slept. Upon awakening, he found his right hand and wrist swollen and in unbearable pain. He had to go to the emergency room, where an x-ray revealed he had broken two bones. A cast was put on his hand for precautionary measures. He was told to stay home for a few days to nurse his hand. But deep inside he wanted to care for the wound of his soul and try to grasp reality and see what he was up against, as he was more convinced than ever to go forward with his relationship with Sophia.

10

The idea of meeting Kevin's mother got Sophia very excited. When she finished the paper she was writing and finally got to Kevin's she was disappointed to find out that Nicole had left prematurely. She wanted to give her a call in order to excuse herself for not speaking to her when she had called Kevin. He convinced her otherwise. However, he had a tougher time explaining why his hand was in a cast. He told her he got hurt at work. But women have a way of knowing when men are lying, especially when those men aren't good at it. She only hoped it had not been a fistfight and that no one was really hurt. Kevin seemed to be preoccupied, but she thought it was one of those days when you just feel drained. She asked him to temporarily cut their social activities to the weekends only so that Kevin could rest a bit more. Kevin did not answer her. He seemed detached and subdued. He had a lot in his mind, including his mother's attitude toward her future daughter-in-law.

The following Thursday, around 5:30, Kevin felt the urge to stop by Sophia's house, because he could not accept the *weekend only* restriction. He rang the bell many times, and he was leaving when Sophia finally opened the door. When he came in, there was a well-dressed gentleman sitting in the living room. Kevin went right by him, looked around and saw that there was no other activity. No TV, no radio on, no other voices to be heard. Seeing no one else, Kevin stood between the dining room and the living room and asked, "Where is everybody else?"

Sophia replied naturally, "Mom and Dad went out."

Kevin walked straight to the gentleman and asked, "Who are you, sir?"

He responded, "I am a friend of the family," while extending his hand for a handshake.

Kevin ignored the hand and continued:

"Friend of the family. Really! That is weird. I have never heard any one talk about you before. I've never seen you before. Do you have a name, dear 'friend of the family'?"

Before the gentleman had a chance to reply, Kevin got closer, pointing his finger at the man's face and said, "Listen buddy, this lady is my fiancée. I love her very much. I would kill for her. Stay away from this place!"

The gentleman turned toward Sophia and said, "Miss Marcel, I guess I'll come back another time."

"There will be no other time," interrupted Kevin. "Stay away from this house; stay away from her, or next time I will not be so pleasant. Now, pick yourself up and get out while you have the chance!"

The gentleman got up, said nothing, walked backward until his hand reached the door knob, opened the door, and walked out.

Kevin ran and locked the door. Sophia was pale, expressionless, angry, humiliated, scared and shocked. She never thought Kevin could be so furious and insane.

Before she had the chance to say a word, Kevin began: "I never understand women. I told you how much I love you. I can't live without you. I will do anything, and I will put up with anything just for you. Don't you understand? People you may not even suspect are not too cheerful about our relationship. But my love for you gets stronger. You told me to take a break, to reduce our time spent together to only weekends. I could not wait that long. I come in and you are engaged in a cordial conversation with another man in your sexy outfit, showing cleavage, while no one else is in the house. What is this? Do you have any explanation? I deserve—I demand an answer, right here, right now."

As tears ran down her cheeks, Sophia did not say one word; she opened the door and told Kevin, "Get out of my house!"

Coincidentally, Bernard and Bertha were coming in. Kevin greeted them.

Sophia said to them, "Let the jerk go."

Bertha asked: "What is going on here, Sophia? I met Mr. John McCauley a couple of blocks away. He was distraught, shaking, and could hardly speak. When I asked him to come back, he told me to talk to you. Here we are, and you are calling Kevin a jerk. Can anybody make some sense out of all this?"

Sophia did not want her parents to see her crying. She ran upstairs, leaving Kevin to deal with the situation.

"Mrs. Marcel, you know that guy who was here?" asked Kevin.

"Of course we know him. He has been our family's insurance agent for years. We called him to review our policies. Unfortunately, we took longer than expected to get back."

Kevin said, "In other words, because you were not home, Sophia welcomed him and was discussing the financial portfolio for the family.

In that case, I really messed up big time. How old is that guy anyway?" asked Kevin.

"He must be in his late fifties" replied Bertha.

"I really blew it!" declared Kevin.

"What do you mean," asked Bertha.

Bernard laughed and said, "Don't tell me you got jealous and made a fool out of yourself."

"That's exactly what happened! How am I going to fix this?"

Bertha said, "Don't worry. It won't be easy, but I think we can handle it."

Bernard replied, "Speak for yourself, and leave me out of this."

"Mrs. Marcel, do you have Mr. McCauley's cell number? I would like to call him and apologize."

"No, Kevin. Go home. Let the dust settle. I will call you later on and tell you how the situation turns out."

Kevin was not too sure which foot to lift first to go home. But, he knew he had a lot of damage control to do.

After Kevin left, he tried to call Sophia at home or on her cell. She did not pick up. So he left a message for her.

At home, dark thoughts assailed Kevin throughout the night. Will Sophia ever forgive me? Why did she ask to see me only on weekends?

Kevin lay face-up in his bed and found himself praying, *Dear Jehovah, I know I have failed you many times. But I also know you are a merciful God. Please help me make the right decision in this situation. The same God who has spared my life in many situations while at war, please help me once again, thank you.* Shortly after, the phone rang, so he got up and answered it. His mother was on the line.

"Hi Kevin!"

"Hello Mother, how are you?"

"I'm okay. I just called to apologize for my behavior the other day. I was in a state of shock; I did not realize what I was saying. I hope you can forgive me."

"I forgive you mother. Right now, I am just confused. I understand where you were coming from."

"Stop that nonsense son. I have no right to come to your house and spoil your happiness the way I did. I hope you can forgive me. I mean it."

"I know you mean it. Thanks for calling. Bye."

"Hold it Kevin. What have I taught you? Didn't I tell you when someone calls you, you must let him or her have the honor of saying goodbye? I am the one who called you."

"OK Mother, you are right. Where are my manners?"

"At any rate, I know you have got to go to work. I won't hold you for long. I just had to get this off my chest. By the way, when is the wedding?"

"I don't know if there will be a wedding!"

"Don't be silly, Son. I saw how happy you were merely mentioning that girl…what's her name again?"

"Sophia, Mother! Sophia!"

"Anyway when you get married, I hope you will invite me."

"Of course, if there is a wedding, I will definitely invite you."

Kevin went to work with flu-like symptoms: malaise, fatigue, light headedness, runny nose—he forced himself to get most of his obligations out of the way, then went back home and slept soundly until three o'clock in the morning. When he got up, he looked at his phone; there were a few text messages from various people, but none from Sophia. He started reading them, but dropped the phone and fell asleep again. The following morning, he was coughing and sneezing, with a runny nose. So he realized it was not psychological. Kevin called his boss to inform him that he was sick. Then he went back to sleep. He stayed in bed all day.

Sophia, at the same time, was upset and puzzled. She had not spoken to Kevin for almost three days. Her parents had convinced her it was a mistake. She knew that Kevin usually got home around four in the afternoon. So by 3:45 she parked right in front of his house to surprise him and also give him a piece of her mind. She stayed there. Nothing happened until 6:30, when she saw Kevin opened his door to get his mail. She blew the horn to get his attention and then got out of the car and walked slowly towards him.

"What is the matter with you?" asked Sophia, very upset.

"I am sick. I am going crazy."

"You can say that again!" replied Sophia. You are sick in your head. I wonder how I can still be talking to you, after the humiliation you put me through!"

"Sophia, I have been asking myself why you stood there and let me make such a fool out of myself the other day.

I would not be surprised if you never spoke to me again. Unfortunately, since then I have been in bed."

"You had better have a doctor's note."

"I am sorry. Please forgive me, won't you?"

Kevin started coughing. Sophia realized he might really be sick. She helped him back to bed. Sophia called her mother. Bertha had always wanted to see the inside of Kevin's home. So she made a pot of her special homemade chicken soup and took it over. Sophia had time to put the apartment in some order before Bertha came. Bertha had intended to stick around, but she figured the guy looked so sick and so frail, she could take a chance and leave— not without first giving to Sophia a significant look that was worth a thousand words, though.

After Bertha left, Kevin took some medicine, ate some soup, showered, and shaved. He looked much better.

Sophia said: "Listen Kevin, trust, respect, and open communication are very important in any relationship. If you feel you cannot trust me, it is not worth going any further."

"You mean to tell me you came all the way here to my house to argue with me? Can't you see I am sick?"

"I am here to see if you are sick in the head!"

"No I'm not. You told me to chill out and I came to see you; and there you were with another man. What did you expect me to think? I got jealous!"

"Are you insecure? Listen, if I did not love you, I would not have hung around with you for so long—"

Sophia continued her monologue: "This is the problem I have with love. It forces you to care, worry, and become possessive—"

"It also makes you feel great. It gives you goose bumps, wings to fly, hope to live, and strength to face any challenges in life," added Kevin.

"So you are choosing when I am sick and weak to tell me that you love me, for the first time?'

"You are always exaggerating, Kevin."

"Hey listen, I was told, in a relationship one should avoid two words—"

"And what are they, Kevin?"

"Always and never."

"Well, listen to this. I was about to tell you I will always love you and will never leave you. I guess I can't say it."

"You know what I mean Sophia. You are such a tease. Listen, I need to ask you for a favor. You must promise me you will grant it."

"I promise you I will consider it carefully," replied Sophia.

"I can't see you on weekends only. I need to see you all the time."

"It's not possible, and you know that, Kevin."

"Listen, let's go back to the usual for now, because once we stop seeing each other as often as we used to, I become sick. I'm a victim of love withdrawal. Am I going to see you tomorrow?"

Sophia took a deep breath and said "Okay. But you know what? I already feel my throat itching. I don't want to get sick right now."

"Oh no! I'm sure you would have a lot of explaining to do to your parents. I can see Mr. Marcel walking back and forth, saying, "Despite all the instructions you give them, they still do not listen. Bertha, can you explain to me how come Sophia got a cold shortly after Kevin was sick? What is going on?"

"Listen Kevin, you look much better. It is getting late. Let me go. I will see you tomorrow." She blew him a kiss and left.

"I will be thinking about you," replied Kevin.

Kevin had no real incentive to get better. His job allowed him to stay home for another week and to give him the chance to see Sophia regularly. But after three more visits at Kevin's house, coincidentally, Bernard wanted to have a talk with Sophia. She already knew what it would likely be about. So she stayed late at school in order to have time to see Kevin. The third night she went there, she felt excited but a bit uncomfortable. The atmosphere was too romantic: some soft music was playing in the background, there was a candlelit dinner, and there was a DVD on the table. Once Kevin started getting too adventurous, she stopped him, told him "no, I am not making that mistake again," and left. But right after she closed that door, she was dying inside. How she wanted to share those feelings also, but she did not think that it was appropriate. She was also grateful that Kevin listened. Had it been Bryan, she did not know what would have happened.

Once she was outside Kevin's apartment, Sophia realized she left her purse on the table with her car keys, and she had no money to get a taxi. She slowly walked down the steps, wondering how on earth she was going to get home. She did not feel like going back to Kevin's apartment. While she was trying to figure out how to get home, Kevin opened the door and yelled,

"You left your keys."

She did not know how or when, but she ended up back in his apartment. She found herself melting into his arms, with kisses, caresses, and sweet words that made her head turn. And just when she felt as if she were about to share an intimate moment, someone knocked suddenly. She quickly rearranged her hair, buttoned her shirt, and opened the door. There was her mother Bertha. She let her have it.

"What is it with you, woman? Don't you have a life? Why do you always have to watch me and follow me like a shadow? I am old enough to make my own decisions. You are making me sick. I have had it with you!"

Sophia almost pushed her away, flew by her and then got in her car and started driving like a madwoman. Bertha was speechless. Kevin was a bit embarrassed. He offered to take her home. But Bertha declined. She pretended she had been in the neighborhood and wanted to bring some home-cooked food for Kevin. She put it on the table. She took a cab and returned home to see Sophia still enraged, taking clothes out of her drawers and putting them in suitcases. Bernard was there looking on, dumbfounded. When Bertha walked in, Sophia said,

"I am moving out before I lose my temper and kill someone!"

Bernard interjected: "Can anyone tell me what is going on?"

Sophia stormed out before Bernard could get any answer.

Bernard said, "I have never seen her so upset in my life. What the devil is getting into her? What did you do this time, Bertha?"

Bertha said, "Don't you start with me! I was young once; I know all the tricks. Can't you see she has been getting home late every night? She has been hanging out with Kevin!"

"So?"

"Bernard, you are not concerned that this young woman is hanging out alone with that young man under no supervision?"

"Listen, at her age there is not much we can do for her. She is an adult. We have taught her everything she needs to know. Now it is up to her. We cannot follow her everywhere. She is grown up. We can only hope and pray that she makes the right decisions; but it is her life; let her handle it."

Bertha said nothing else for the remainder of the evening. The house was silent. Were they worried about Sophia's safety? Were they upset with each other? Did Bertha believe she made a mistake, or was she right? The next sound was the alarm clock at six the following morning. Bernard shut it off. Both remained in bed a bit later than usual, wondering what happened to Sophia.

At nine, Kevin called, asking for her. They realized he did not know her whereabouts either. They told him she was not available. She would call him back. But Bernard and Bertha were both relieved, knowing she did not sleep under the same roof with Kevin.

Kevin woke up with a sour taste in his mouth and a feeling of indigestion. He was not too happy about what happened the night before. He could not fully understand Sophia's reaction, yet somewhat he was glad that she gave her parents some limits. He always thought they were too possessive and needed to let her loose to make her own decisions and have her own experiences.

While he tried to figure out why he felt bruised, he remained puzzled by Sophia's behavior. He had never felt so much in love. He could not stop thinking of her and dreaming about her. He wanted to share her company all the time. He was also convinced the feeling was mutual. Somehow he loved the fact she was completely in charge of her life. This challenge attracted him even more. Before he left for his daily errands, he wrote Sophia an email message telling her how much he loved her and could not live without her. He asked to meet her in the park at five a few blocks from her college.

They met and fell into passionate embraces and kisses; each felt like lifting each other to high places. Hand in hand they went for a long cordial walk. They talked about Sophia's parents. Kevin agreed she should go back home, at least for a short while, but she must set some clear conditions.

Shortly before that special day of their one year anniversary together, Kevin asked Sophia to go out with him for a special evening. She was very excited about the idea but she was a bit under the weather, so she wanted to put it off for another time. Kevin did not seem to be insistent. Sophia had been back home for a while. One Sunday morning around eleven, Kevin came into the house and handed her a pound of fish. He was smiling nervously. He asked her if she would cook it for him. She found this quite odd. He sure had been acting strange lately.

> "Hey sir! What's happening to you? You don't even greet me? I thought you came early to celebrate our one year together. But, it seems that you forgot!"
>
> "Forgive me darling. I was dying to see you. I did not realize it was so early. Are you okay? You told me you were not feeling too well. I can't wait for the time when I can personally take care of you."
>
> "I am okay, thanks! It is so nice to see you."
>
> "By the way, you look even more beautiful in your pajamas. I feel so good when I see those eyes; it is like the moon shining down on my path. Your smile is like the morning sunrise on a spring day—"
>
> "Kevin, my dear, I thank you for all your kind words. You know I love you. You look very handsome yourself. Isn't it a little early on a Sunday morning?"
>
> "Sophia, my love, I could not sleep; I kept thinking about you. So—"

Sophia kissed him. They tenderly hugged one another, and said goodbye.

Sophia put the fish in the sink and went back to her room, fantasizing. Before Kevin stepped out, he made sure he told Bertha to let her daughter handle the fish. Around two o'clock, Sophia finally came down and tried to prepare the fish. As she opened the fish's mouth, a half-carat diamond ring was glistening at her.

> She screamed at the top of her lungs: "He did it! He did it!" She left everything in the sink and ran up to her parents: "Mom, Dad, Kevin did it! He did it!"
>
> "He did what?" asked Bernard and Bertha simultaneously. But she could only repeat herself: "He did it!" She took them to the sink and they saw the ring.
>
> "This is beautiful!" exclaimed her mother. "I have never seen anything so beautiful. This is expensive. This must cost over $5,000. Wow! Congratulations, Sophia."

Bertha was happy for her daughter and started singing, *Here comes the bride…* She hugged Sophia again with tears of joy streaming down her cheeks. Sophia noted that her dad said almost nothing but was in deep thought. He looked concerned, but she was too thrilled to say anything at that time, hoping it was because her Dad was in a state of shock. Kevin had it all planned out. That evening, Sophia's family hosted a dinner for Kevin and his mother, who flew in shortly before, just for that special occasion. On his knees and in front of the few gathered, Kevin popped the question officially: "Sophia, will you marry me?" She said, "Yes," without a second thought. Kevin and Sophia were officially engaged, with the wedding date to be determined. Yet Bernard said very little. The party ended a bit late. Everybody was very happy, including Nicole.

12

Monday was a holiday. Bernard, who was usually pretty busy, stayed in his room all day and hardly made a sound. By five o'clock, the family gathered around the table. As usual, Bernard sat at the head of the table. This time he asked Junior to say grace, and everybody ate with little conversation. Bertha made a few comments about the beauty of Sophia's ring.

Junior quipped, "That's nothing! It is probably fake."

Sophia accused Junior of being "…jealous and unable to appreciate nice things."

Bernard had still said very little. After the meal, Junior excused himself, pretending to have a business meeting. Bernard excused himself as well. This time Sophia followed him into his study for a talk.

"Dad, what is going on with you? I noticed you are a bit dazed, subdued. What is bugging you? Shouldn't you be happy for me?"

"Yes I am very happy for you!"

Sophia continued, "But—"

"Do you want to put words into my mouth?"

"No, but I know you, and I know you have something you are holding back. I want to hear it!"

"Are you sure you want to hear it? Can you handle it without getting upset?"

"Dad, tell me, is it the race issue?"

"Have you ever discussed that with him?"

"Yes! Kevin and I see people as human beings. Love should be colorblind."

"Is it? The fact that someone is concerned about a mixed, interracial marriage does not necessarily mean he or she is prejudiced, or that he or she hates other people. In an ideal world, people see and judge others based on their character, personality, performance, and contribution to the human race. However, this is not a perfect world that we are living in. People are biased. All of us have preferences. All of us discriminate, meaning we choose based on our preferences. We are all somewhat biased. I am not talking about bigotry. I am talking about convenience, what the society sees as normal, and what is expected. There is the stereotype, people's reactions to a mixed couple, and the challenges for offspring."

"Dad, let's stay focused. What are you trying to tell me? We are not talking about the world, society, regimes, the system, the government; we are talking about the life of Sophia, your daughter. What is it that you want to say?"

"Have a seat, my dear."

Sophia sat. Bertha came in and sat in Bernard's chair. Bernard walked back and forth as if to find the best way to convey his apprehension without giving his daughter the wrong impression. Leaning against the window, his eyes gazing away from hers, he began in a soft and low voice:

"Sophia, it is all parents' dream to see their children grow up, become self-sufficient, have a career and a family. It is very exciting for parents to see their daughter fall in love for real and decide to get married. I can tell you we are happy for you. Personally, as a father, of course I have mixed feelings to be sorted out. But your mother and I have a specific concern that most parents do not have: you are embarking on an interracial marriage. As you look at us—your mother and me—you know that marriage is not easy. It requires a lot of understanding, respect, common beliefs, values, and everlasting commitments. But to add the race issue into it can be quite a task. I have no doubt you can handle it, but—"

"What does Kevin's mother say about this?" interrupted Bertha.

"She has some issues about it but agrees that it is Kevin's call," replied Sophia.

Bernard said, "As I was saying, you can decide to marry anyone based on your criteria and your judgment. You cannot put barriers around love. Your heart can guide you in synchrony with your brain. Race should not be a single determinant in your choice. Everyone who is looking for a lasting relationship should go according to some basic determinants. What is it that makes you decide to marry someone outside of your race and culture? What is behind such a choice? Is it a rejection of your people or prejudice against them? Is it to get even? Is it low self-esteem? Is it to affirm yourself against what you were taught? Is it—"

"Dad, with all due respect, may I remind you we are talking about me and Kevin, nobody else. Kevin came after me, I felt his sincerity, and I was very reluctant.

Many times I was even unfair to him. I challenged him often. But he proved to be true. He is a gentleman, and he is sensitive, caring, respectful, trustworthy, committed, humble, mature, stable, considerate, reliable, and well mannered. Kevin has everything that a woman could dream of. I have fallen in love with him, and I am convinced that we are compatible. And we love each other. He is my soulmate. We share common values and common goals. He makes me laugh, and he makes me happy. I never felt this way before. Now, are you saying I should put my heart in a box and tell it to exclude Kevin just because he is white? Do you think I can force my heart as to where and when to express its love and to whom? You told me long ago that before race, we are all human beings sharing the same emotions, sentiments, and feelings. Am I to limit those same feelings to exclude Kevin? Are you saying I should worry more about people's stereotype, comments, reactions, and even bigotry before my own well-being? What is this? Is this a case of national security? Is this a sin, or a moral issue? Oh God! What am I hearing here?"

Bertha put her hand around her daughter and said softly, "Your dad is trying very hard to convey the dilemma and the complexity of this world—"

Sophia pulled away gently and said "Everyone keeps blaming the world for all evil, all unfairness. But do you realize that the world is made up of people? Some people should take a stance and stop accepting the world as it is and start showing how it should be."

"Let me say one last word on that subject," interjected Bernard, "Over a century ago our great-grandparents were slaves. My dad told me about my great-grandpa. He was a young man, the youngest of seven brothers and two sisters. He was taken away from his mother, who was not allowed to take care of him. Living on a plantation, he was a dedicated, strong, tireless worker who initially made the owner very happy. From four o'clock in the morning, until eleven at night, he was working, serving, helping, and whatever else he was asked to do. The owner, Mr. Mattock, was married and had a daughter who was to be married. But one night, the family left for an important gathering. The daughter, Lydia, told everyone at the last minute she was sick and urged them to go and leave her home to rest. In the middle of the night, somehow Lydia came to my great grandpa's room, and the rest was history. Lydia still got married. But when she gave birth months later, it was a black baby. This was a horrible act. Dad's grandpa was lynched. Lydia's mother managed to save the life of the baby by sending him out of state. This is how our history began. Grandpa never knew his dad. He grew up on a place that was large enough to have many servants, and he was one of them. He had to work very hard. The others were always making fun of him. Some even called him Mr. White, because he was light skinned. They said he did not walk, talk, or reason like them. He always wanted to do more in life. They thought he wanted to be the best in everything, and he did. He always thought if one human being could do it, he could do it too. They resented him for that. There he was, rejected by his own people, and he was mistreated by the white folks. He managed to cope. He learned to put words together and make sense out of them while the children in the house were doing their homework. He was a determined, gifted young man. He was always among the first to finish his task and to help others. This is how he met Grandma, another servant, who saw in him a beacon of hope and a man of character. Although she was under all kinds of pressure and wearing used clothes, he saw her inner beauty. To make a long story short, they got together and worked hard to create a better life for their children. This is how they outdid themselves for my education and got me to be who I am today."

"I am sorry for that tragedy, Dad. But this is another reason to break those barriers. Times have changed. Look around you, even in the White House! Things are different now. I know we still see open or subtle prejudice and rejection, but if any couple can make it out there, Kevin and I are going to be the one. True love can conquer all."

"Change will not come easily or quickly. Centuries of hurt, mistreatment, mistrust will not fade away overnight. Anyway, I am very glad you feel that way. And your mother and I wish you all the best," said Bernard.

They hugged each other, and everyone retired to their rooms.

13

Several weeks had passed since Kevin popped the question of engagement to his beloved Sophia. Sophia graduated college and got a job as a paralegal so she could save for law school. Life became more settled. Sophia continued to make arrangements in her mind for a committed lifestyle—and for her wedding. She had beauty, youth and family support, she was healthy, she was working, and she was in love. Who could ask for anything more? To Sophia, it all seemed too beautiful to be true.

One afternoon, with Bernard out of town presenting motivational conferences, Sophia came home earlier than usual, and Bertha decided to have another heart-to-heart talk with her daughter.

"Hello, Sophia. How are things going?" asked Bertha.

"Things are going great, Mom!"

"How is Kevin? Is he behaving?"

"What do you mean, Mom? You never asked me that before."

"I had no reason to inquire before. But these days, I just think I should ask. When people are engaged, things that can happen do happen."

"Everything is fine, Mom. By the way, can I ask you a personal question?"

"Sure! Go ahead, shoot!"

"Did you ever get intimate before you were married?"

Bertha was taken a bit off guard. Her faced dropped, she took a deep breath, sat down with Sophia, and began.

"Are you sure you have the stomach to take what I am about to tell you? This is serious stuff that very few people know, and I hope they have forgotten it—"

"Come on Mom, go ahead!"

"Well! I was young, beautiful, sure of myself and full of pride. Everywhere I went guys were after me. My parents were very strict. Dad would always remind me that I was a pastor's daughter. But I was very rebellious."

"Mom, you were rebellious? I find that hard to believe," interrupted Sophia.

"Listen, the main difference between then and now is the options, what is available, the choices," replied Bertha. "We had no internet, Facebook, cell phones, and iPods. But teenagers are teenagers. Anyway, I was very choosy, pretentious, and even arrogant. Then along came Bill Meyers, six-feet-two, with a little puppy mustache. He was a hockey player and I was star struck."

"How did you meet him, Mom?"

"I was away on campus. Toward the end of our freshman year, we were having a party in the gymnasium. I bumped into him and dropped a cup of hot chocolate on him. To make a long story short, we made up. It was love at first sight. I wouldn't listen to anyone. Bill was fast and apparently experienced. Before you knew it, it was one moment, one hot spring evening, and I melted. I let my guard down and that was it. A few weeks later, I was pregnant."

"What?! You mean to tell me that Bertha Preston got

pregnant out of wedlock by a man she hardly knew. Mom! Are you sure about that? Or is this something you thought had happened to you? I can't believe my ears. My own mother, the pastor's daughter, was impregnated by a man other than my dad."

Then came a long pause between them. Bertha sat down and her voice was cracking, her eyes became watery. Sophia held her hand. She added, "I am sorry Mom. Do you want to stop or can you continue?"

"Well, there isn't much left anyway. I was ignorant. My parents would not even think about talking to me about love and sex. These topics were taboo at home."

"So what happened Mom?"

"He disappeared from the scene.—"

"He did what?" asked Sophia

"He vanished. I was devastated. I even thought about committing suicide. I was becoming crazy, literally. I could not talk to anyone, fearing my dad would know. I could not let him down like that. I was losing weight, vomiting…I became pale. The worst part, I had no one to talk to. I could not trust anyone. I did not know where to find any help. Then one day, as I was sitting alone on a bench, your father approached me. He told me he knew everything and he was there to help me."

"My Dad did that! How did he know?"

"Later on he told me he thought something happened to me but he did not really know the facts. So by telling me he knew, I opened my heart to him and told him what my situation was."

"What did he say?"

"He told me—with the same calm you see in him now,

'don't worry I will take care of everything.' Yes! Bernard Marcel, a young adolescent, stepped forward and came to my rescue."

"How did he do that?"

"He was always interested in me. He was a gentleman, the reserved type. He would write me little poems, send me cards, and walk with me on campus. But he was not the type to fight over a girl. So, after my big tragedy, I was flat and doomed. He approached me and told me he thought something was wrong with me. I was different. I was 'less cheerful' (those were his words). He had always been genuinely caring. He insisted so much. So, I explained to him the situation. Do you know what he said?"

"What did he say, Mom?"

"He told me 'Don't worry about it; I will marry you'— with the calm and certitude that he always had. I did not think he knew what he was saying, nor could I believe my ears. Besides, I did not want to be married. I did not want him to have pity on me."

"Say what? You mean to tell me he took responsibility for the pregnancy, even though he was not the father? My dad did that? Now I know why you always look up to him. He is your hero."

"He was a very bright young man. In our girls' talks, we talked about him a lot. But we were scared of him. He was too serious. Nevertheless, through this darkest moment of my life, he revealed himself to be an angel. He told me I should not have an abortion. We were not clear how to handle it to endure the least amount of rejection and blame, but he was prepared to get the wrath of my parents and his for something he did not do. A few weeks later, before our arranged marriage to save face, some friends and I were just driving around, we got rear ended. Right after that car accident I developed severe abdominal pain. I was rushed into the hospital. They could not save the baby—"

"I am so sorry, Mom!"

"There was another dilemma," added Bertha. Your dad told me 'we lost someone who could have grown to become an Einstein.' Anyway, it took a while before we could go on with our lives. It is so painful to suffer and not be able to tell others because the reason can't be shared. People look at you. You look weird in their eyes. They ask you how things are. All you can say is 'all right,' while you are dying inside. The pain is so intense it keeps you mute."

"You can say that again!"

"After such a trauma, we had mixed feelings. There were times I was in a terrible mood, feeling sad, depressed, and guilty. He would be quiet, withdrawn. I guess both of us mourned the death of the unborn baby in our own way. He went through all my mood swings with courage and perseverance. I really fell in love with him. He is a wonderful man. Finally we decided to take our time and then got married later on when we were ready. My love for Bernard flows naturally, and I believe it is mutual. He taught me what love really is. He showed me how to love. He gave me hope, and self-confidence. You see, Sophia, when you get too far it is very hard to stop. Then you have a guilty conscience. Everything that happens in your life, you tend to blame on your past mistakes. As a woman, I believe it is our call to decide when to do what. You should have rules and values and set limits early, firmly but gently."

"Boy that was a close call! Did you ever tell your parents?"

"Not immediately but later, when everything was settled. The lesson to learn from that terrible experience of mine is that you should recognize your feelings. It is normal to have an irresistible desire to be intimate with your partner, especially in your situation. But think it through. Give it time. Do not rush, and do not put yourself in any vulnerable situation where you cannot undo what is done. I know this is a new world, a new generation, with new ideas, new definitions, and even new concepts of what is right or wrong. But time will tell. The call is yours. I trust you to make the right decision."

"Wow! This is heavy stuff. Thank you for sharing this with me."

14

Bernard and Bertha had been married for years. But anytime they argued it was usually about the same issues. Bertha always wanted him to do things he didn't like to do, including going shopping. They would agree to go to the stores and markets, and Bernard would stay in the car. However, sooner or later Bertha would drag him into the stores to come and look, and then the same arguments started. Bertha enjoyed spending time in the malls. She called it her shopping therapy. Bernard was just the opposite. One particular Sunday afternoon was no exception. Bernard was not feeling too well. He felt a bit sluggish but with no specific pain. He would never complain. So Bertha kept nagging him. Finally, he told Bertha: "Tell you what, once I am done washing and cleaning the car, I will take you to the beauty parlor and get you off my case."

Knowing that Bernard was about to take his sweet time as usual, Bertha went inside the house to watch some TV. She fell asleep right in front of the TV. In the meantime, Bernard decided to change his oil. Bertha woke up startled by the noise and commotion of an ambulance, the police, and the fire department stopping right in front of her house. Mr. Bernard Marcel was removed from under his car, motionless, and taken by ambulance to the nearest hospital. "What happened?" Bertha kept asking, but no one really knew. He was found face up, his feet under the car. How did it happen? Even Mr. Marcel himself could not explain. He had a full work-up with no conclusive diagnosis. They believed he fainted from exhaustion. Maybe he was sweating too much in the heat while trying to jack up the car. He might have passed out. He took it easy for a few days. But six weeks later he was cleared by his cardiologist. So he resumed his public speaking engagements. Nobody could stop Bernard, anyway. Bertha said he was stubborn like a mule. He called Bertha the drama queen.

15

Sophia returned home after a difficult day at work, frustrated and tired. As she entered the house, Bertha greeted her:

"Hello dear! Guess what, I keep getting calls from guys who are trying to be friendly with me once I tell them you are my daughter."

"Really! That's news to me. Who are they? Did you take any messages?"

"No. They all seem reluctant to leave a message."

"Listen, Mom, if someone is really significant in my life, business or otherwise, he or she would have my cell phone number. So, don't worry about them."

"Sophia, you are currently engaged to be married in six months; this is a golden opportunity to get everything that is humanly possible under control and to avoid gross surprises."

"Of course mother! I have everything under control. What is it that you are trying to tell me?"

"Everybody must know by now that Kevin and you are fully committed to each other. Nowadays, you must remain vigilant and not let your guard down. Everyone must know officially, including Bryan or any other possible secret admirers of yours."

Sophia laughed. "Mom, you mean I should walk around with a sign on my forehead that says 'TAKEN'?"

"Don't be silly, Sophia. Again, it is normal to share and express your love with someone. But it is a private affair at the right time in the right place. You must set limits and stay in control. That's all I can tell you, based on your learned values. Do not feel pressured to accommodate because it is convenient. The key question is: Are you ready? Do you know all the consequences? Have you met the requirements?"

Sophia who was usually talkative and ready to express herself did not seem willing to venture into more questions or revelations. As she was involved in some deep thinking, Bertha realized she may have come across a bit too strong and therefore she excused herself.

Sophia went to check her email; she found one from her Dad that read:

> *My beloved daughter, I have a few minutes to spare, I thought I would chit-chat a bit with you. How are you? It just dawned upon me that Saturday is your birthday. Now that you are engaged, you are one step away from marriage. I feel the urgency to help you navigate this stage with confidence and cast away the possible doubts.*
>
> *The main threshold about marriage, besides love, is maturity. Maturity allows you to face the music and to dance accordingly. One can preach about maturity, recite its definition left and right; however, it is something that is reflected in your choices, your character, and your behavior.*
>
> *I would not be surprised if you were asking yourself the key question: am I ready to get married?*

Allow me to suggest a checklist:

*1. Am in love? Do I love him? Does he love me?
People love each other when they are attracted
to each other not only physically but also by
shared values, interests, and goals. They invest
time to learn about each other. They are able
and willing to take steps to make each other
happy, and to promote growth, self reliance, trust,
and individual success. They respect each other,
they are considerate, and they have the ability
to communicate and resolve conflicts without
constant bickering and cursing. They are willing
to spend time with each other, to adjust, and to
secure and protect each other. They are responsible
and caring.*

*2. Despite being head over heels in love, can you
stand each other day in and day out? Are both of
you marriage material?*

*Ideally, all of us wish to meet people who are not
selfish, irresponsible, inconsiderate, lazy, querulous,
pathologically jealous, abusive, insecure, or
flirtatious, moody, or rude. Nevertheless, we need
to learn to adjust and accept people as they are.*

*3. What are your weaknesses, and what are his?
How can the two of you cope and adjust?
Bear in mind, there are some patterns
inherent to men, and others inherent to
women. Do you understand the man's needs;
does he understand the woman's needs?*

*4. What is the family plan? Career, goals, aspirations,
children, where to live, how many children, how
to raise them? Married name: yours or his?*

5. What is the role of spirituality, religion?

6. What is the viewpoint about sex?

7. What about finances? Debt management? Savings? Investments?

All in all, two people know they are ready to get married when they approach such a step convinced that they are in love with each other, they know enough about each other, and are willing to stay committed for life. The intent is very important. They want and can trust each other. They maintain their independence in thinking and are allowed to mutually make decisions that are best for the family. They have nothing to hide from society or each other. They are willing to work, respect, care, and do whatever is necessary to preserve the union. They are mutually willing and able to perform sexually. They should be humble enough to learn about conjugal life and get counseling from experts who share their values and are worthy of their trust and confidence, if needed.

Enough said for today. I'll talk to you soon.

Love,

Dad.

Sophia went to a few other emails, talked to Kevin on the phone forever, and then fell asleep.

16

It was April first, and Sophia was in Alabama for business; she received a phone call around six o'clock in the morning. Kevin woke her up, forgetting there was a one-hour time difference between New York and Alabama.

"Hello baby, did I wake you up? I'm sorry."

"That's okay, Kevin. What's on your mind?"

Kevin hesitated a few seconds and then said "nothing special. I wanted to tell you that I may go out of town for a while."

"What are you talking about, Kevin? Is everything okay? Is your mother all right? What's going on?"

"Everything is fine. There have been some changes in my work schedule and assignment. That's all."

"What changes? What are you trying to say?"

"Nothing to worry yourself about, sweetheart! On April first, you shouldn't take me too seriously. When you come back tomorrow, we will discuss it. Again, don't worry yourself. Everything is fine. I love you. Have a good day; we will talk later."

"I love you, too. I miss you so much. Hugs and kisses. Talk to you soon."

They hung up. Yet Sophia felt uncomfortable. She spent the day pondering the call. Kevin's voice sounded a bit concerned. He was not as cheerful as usual. What could be the reason? She did her best to imagine all kinds of possibilities. Despite some gut feelings, and some vague intuition, she officially remained clueless.

Night came and the two talked for a long time. Kevin, after the morning call, realized he made a mistake. So he decided to play it down. The dialogue focused on love and sweet things here and there. Sophia finally realized nothing was going to be told until she was physically there, so she gave up, hoping to get home early enough to catch up on the latest events. Her flight to New York was delayed for four hours. She arrived home at one in the morning. She went straight to bed. Early the following morning, on Saturday, Kevin came to see her. He tried to be as cheerful as possible. They talked about mundane things and reaffirmed their love for each other. Then Kevin stood up in the living room and said, "What I am about to tell you is not going to be pleasant. Please, brace yourself."

"What is it, Kevin? Do you want to get out of the engagement? You have got cold feet six months before the wedding, is that it? Go ahead; I am a tough girl I can take that punch. It will be hard, very hard, but I will survive."

"Sophia, stop being silly. You know I will always love you."

"But…so what is it Kevin? Do you have a child? Do you have another woman? Do you have a disease?"

"Sophia, please, let me finish, this is a very serious matter to both of us."

"That's it! You are going back to the war zone? Aren't you?"

As tears ran down Sophia's cheeks, Kevin said, "My dear, my love for you is unquestionable. Nevertheless, I have a bigger love—the love for my country. Right now I am being called upon once again to help my country, and I cannot say no."

"What do you mean you cannot say no? What happens to all the other people who have not served yet? I thought you said your contract was over."

"Sophia, please sit down, be quiet, and listen for heaven's sake."

Sophia sat down sobbing. Mom and Dad's door remained cracked open—they could hear the conversation. Kevin took a deep breath and began:

"In this life on earth, one cannot have everything he wants. After I met you again, after you said yes to me, I thought I was in paradise. But it was too beautiful to be real. We are engaged to be married October 15, on my birthday. I have to earn a living. My current job is only temporary; the economy is not doing great, at least for me. People are getting laid off, I can't wait for that to happen. In the army, not only do I get a good and secure job, I also have the great satisfaction that I am serving my country. What greater honor than to be able to defend our beloved country against those bastards who are jealous of us and relentlessly want to attack us? I believe I have a personal calling to put my country first. After so many weeks of trying to find something permanent and substantial, I re-enlisted for another year. They promised me I was not going to be deployed again. Unfortunately, the situation on the ground has changed. We need more manpower. I wish those politicians would have enough courage to return with the draft. But in the meantime the duty is upon us to defend this country. On behalf of all those who die, including my own dad, I intend to return to duty."

"I know a lot of great and secure jobs, but going to combat is not one of them. How could you sign without even consulting with me? When did all that happen, anyway?"

"Two days ago, the morning I talked to you. I got a call from Sergeant Woodmeir, and he told me to return to duty and to be ready for redeployment by next week after all the preliminaries."

"Kevin, you knew all that—why did you come after me, to capture my heart, and now to leave it in a sling? Why did you do that?"

"I am sorry you feel that way. My love for you is unquestionable. I do not imagine having a meaningful existence without you by my side. This is a fact. Unfortunately, life is so unpredictable. I believe the same God who was with me in the past will still be with me. I will return after helping my country in such a critical war. Whatever happens, rest assured, I never loved anyone like you and I never will."

Sophia pulled him down. He sat beside her on the sofa. With head on his shoulders, she asked him: "WHY?"

Kevin did not know what this *why* meant. So he said nothing, while caressing her soft dark hair and drying her eyes with his kisses. Then Kevin asked her a question:

"I need to report for duty in three days; why don't you marry me now?"

She pulled away, stood up and said: "Just like that?" Sophia asked.

After a short moment of reflection, Sophia said "No sir, I am not rushing into a marriage when I do not see any future at this moment. Let us wait and see. I am just curious, what made you think of such an idea at a moment like this? What are you after?"

"Why not get married? I want to seal my love for you I want a complete hold of my wife. Why not, baby?"

"What if you do not come back? Then I am a young widow. With my luck I would get pregnant with a baby who will grow up without ever knowing his father. Can you imagine the heartache, the agonizing pain, or even the anger of a child searching restlessly for a father figure, looking for a mentor in every shadow he or she sees? I can see it is still painful for you even to talk about it. As much as it is possible, I do not want to do that to my child."

"I do not understand you. I do not understand you at all. You tend to dramatize things and expect the worst. Why can't you think positively? You just jinxed me, you know! The other side of the coin is that we can be married and spend two nights together. Who says anything about getting pregnant? This is the twenty-first century—"

"You are a despicable, typical man! Even at such a tragic time, you still have one thing on your mind, don't you?"

"Sophia, baby, you are becoming unreasonable, unyielding…for once, be spontaneous! Why does everything have to be planned and written down? To run your life like a script is boring."

"You just found out that I am boring! There are more surprises where this comes from. So you'd better quit while you are ahead."

Sophia attempted to leave him alone in the living room. He gently held her and kissed her and again told her, "Today I discovered I love you more even when you are angry. You are so charming."

"Leave me alone!"

"Why don't you come to spend the day with me, just this once? Show me that you love me truly. Won't you feel bad if I die when you realize you do not have a total souvenir of me?"

"Kevin, you are using the guilt line; it won't work with me. You can't imagine how I feel, right now!"

"Come with me baby! Please!" I know you feel the same way. Let us not miss that opportunity—"

As Kevin continued to persuade Sophia with the sweet seducing sound of his voice, with sugar-coated words along with some delicate touching, Junior popped up as if he did not know that any one was in the living room.

"Excuse me!" exclaimed Junior sarcastically.

Kevin and Sophia pulled away from each other. Kevin greeted Junior warmly as usual, then said goodbye, hoping that Sophia would pay him a visit.

Kevin left, and Sophia landed in her parents' room crying her heart out. Junior rushed into the room and said, "I didn't mean to hurt your feelings, sis!"

Bernard and Bertha gently told Junior to go take care of his business.

After weeping for a while, Bertha got closer to her.

She said, "Sophia, your Dad and I heard everything. We empathize with you. Right now everything is upside down in your head. You do not know what to do. But you are strong; you are going to pull through it. We are here to support you every step of the way."

"You see Mom, this is exactly why I did not want to fall in love again. I did not want to get committed and be hurt again."

"I am sorry darling, but trust me, you are getting stronger. Sophia whatever we can do to help you go through this separation, we will," interjected Bernard.

Sophia isolated herself in her room for the entire day. Even her food had to be brought to her by her mother.

Bernard and Bertha spent a great deal of time discussing whether or not Sophia should marry Kevin before he left. Bertha was for the marriage, Bernard was against it. There was no consensus.

Kevin spent the day hoping she would visit him or call him; she did not. The following day, Kevin called before stopping by; Sophia did not return his call. When he called Bertha to tell her he was leaving for duty in two days, Bertha decided, on her own, to prepare a special dinner for him and even told him to invite a few friends over. That Tuesday evening, Sophia decided to give up. She wanted to give it all to the man she loved. After she left work, she did not even want to go to her own house and see her parents. She had it all planned out: she would stop by Lakota's place to freshen up and then drive to Kevin's apartment. She had the key; she wanted to surprise him. Unfortunately, Kevin was not there. Everything was already packed up in the apartment. She fixed the place up. She cleaned the kitchen, bathroom, living room and bedroom, while wondering if this is the kind of husband he was going to be, putting socks, underwear and everything all over the place. After she finished making the apartment acceptable and orderly, she noticed it was already 9:00 o'clock. She called him to find out where he was. He told her he was with some friends. He would see her later on. Sophia felt like telling him not to bother. She hung up. She left a note: '…you missed your chance!' and drove home. When she arrived, there was the party organized by her own mother without her prior knowledge. Sophia did not know if she should blast them all off or ignore them all. She took a deep breath, politely said hi to everyone, and carried on a conversation as if nothing happened. Bertha took the liberty to introduce her daughter as "Kevin's fiancée." Everyone applauded. Kevin's best friend Joseph offered some special congratulations. Sophia said "thank you," when in fact she wanted to tell all of them to go to hell. The party went on until early in the morning. Kevin and his friends came together in an SUV. They excused themselves politely. They waited for Kevin for a few minutes to say his long romantic goodbyes. Sophia accompanied him to the door of the truck. They shared their last embrace. As Kevin got in the truck, she said "Bye. You don't know what you missed." From the bedroom Bernard and Bertha waved goodbye "May God be with you!" exclaimed Bernard. Sophia stood outside until the SUV completely disappeared. Kevin was not sure he heard correctly what he thought he heard until he got home and saw her note on the refrigerator. Before he knew it, five o'clock was upon him. He had to go; the other comrades were waiting outside. He put everything in the truck and as they were about to pull away, Bernard, Bertha, and Sophia came to say another goodbye. It was heart-wrenching. Everyone was so moved as they departed from each other. It was a long drive back to the Marcel's residence. Those thirty minutes were longer than eternity. Bertha was behind the wheel, and Sophia sat in the back. It felt like coming out of a funeral service. Not a sound came out of anybody's mouth. Yet everyone seemed to think they knew what the other was thinking. Every now and then, Bertha would take a look at her daughter through the rearview mirror. Bernard would turn around once in a while. Yet Sophia ignored them. Her eyes were closed. As they approached their destination it started pouring heavily for several minutes. Bertha blurted out, "Can you believe this? It took only one phone call, one stupid phone call to ruin everything!" Bernard approved by his look. Finally the rain stopped and the sun appeared. Bertha said, "Isn't it strange, a few minutes ago it was thunder, rain, and darkness. Now, the sun is already saying good morning. This is to tell us that dark moments don't last forever. After the rain, the sunshine will come."

Sophia gathered her strength to pick herself up and get out of the car to go back to her room. Before closing the door, she said "Don't worry guys, I'll be all right." As she passed through the living room, she heard the radio playing from the basement, *I Dreamed A Dream* from *Les Misérables*. She went into her room and shut the door.

Despite all appearances of being very courageous, deep inside, Sophia was being eaten alive by hurt and anger. Six months away from the biggest moment in her life, the moment that almost every girl dreams of, and she was denied such a privilege. She became angry, short-tempered, and withdrawn. Because she had such a good boss, she was granted a few days off. But staying home with her mother drove her crazy. The mother–daughter rivalry resurfaced. The arguments became more and more frequent, to the point that Dad was planning to send his wife to her sister's until the storm died down. After Kevin reached his final destination, the two lovebirds began to email each other daily, sometimes more than once, along with occasional phone calls whenever it was feasible. Sophia resigned herself to take things as they came on a daily basis, hoping for the best but mentally preparing herself for the worst. Love across the ocean was rough. Long-distance relationships are a challenge. Nevertheless both of them swore to remain committed, engaged to be married once Kevin's tour of duty in Iraq was over. He even promised her that this time he would not renew his contract, while she promised she would support both of them until he happened to find another job. He took advantage of any circumstances to send or order souvenirs and gifts for her. However, nothing could replace his actual physical being. They kept hoping somehow things would get better. They wished the war would be over and all the soldiers would return home safely to their families. Sophia wanted to become an activist for peace and wished everyone would jump on the bandwagon for peace. This was a source of disagreement at home when Dad began to point out that no one could have peace unless he or she was willing to pay the price, face the evil forces head on, and destroy them.

October came and went without a wedding. The Christmas holiday was approaching, and Kevin managed to schedule a two-week leave. He reiterated his desire to marry Sophia during that short window of opportunity. Sophia missed him so much and was not sure what would happen when the two of them would meet for those two weeks. So she informed her parents. Dad said no, Mom said yes. Sophia decided to go for it!

It was a week before Christmas; there were a lot of activities all over town. That Wednesday was strangely quiet. No emails, no text messages, no phone calls. Sophia thought preparations for leave or even actual travel could somehow explain the situation. There are times in your life when you choose to believe in an illusion just to nurture hope or avoid facing the reality life imposes on you. Sophia was even scared to talk about it. That Wednesday night, the phone rang. Sophia picked it up on the first ring. "Hello Kevin!"

After short pause, a more mature voice responded "No, it is not Kevin, this is Sergeant Woodmeir—"

"What happened to Kevin?" Sophia asked impatiently.

"Nothing! I mean he is alive, except he had a little accident."

"A little accident, what do you mean?" Sophia started screaming on the phone.

Bernard rushed in picked up the phone, and Sergeant Woodmeir explained that Kevin was on a Humvee that went into a land mine; he was somehow projected away but did not die. They were currently evaluating the extent of his injuries and would give an updated report as soon as it was available.

"Sergeant, can you give me your word that he is not dead?"

"He is not dead. The preliminary report revealed that he is in good shape and good spirits. When I got the bulletin, he was in a state of shock, but his vital signs were stable. He is about to go for an exploratory laparoscopy and a few other routine procedures. These are routine tests to make sure the extent of the injury is known and contained, and that everything is under control."

"What about those who were with him?" asked Bernard.

"I am not in a position to discuss the others with strangers, sir. The fact is Kevin is likely going to make it."

They hung up. Bernard told Sophia to calm down. She remained restless for the entire night. The following morning, after the dust settled, the final news was: Kevin broke one arm and one leg and suffered from minor burns. His condition was stable. He was not likely to suffer permanent physical damage from such trauma. In the meantime, Sophia felt ill. She remained secluded in her room for days with a minimum amount of food and water. After a few days she had to be taken to the hospital, where they decided to keep her because of dehydration and shock and anxiety. By the third day, she was able to speak to Kevin. She was discharged shortly after. Slowly, Sophia bounced back, after Kevin resumed his regular conversations on the phone with her, telling her what had happened. He was going to be all right, and he told her he loved and missed her very much.

In the meantime, one of Kevin's companions, Joseph, who returned earlier from duty, did not make matters easier. Upon arriving in town, he started visiting Sophia regularly. He appointed himself as a liaison between Kevin and Sophia. But instead of reassuring her, he kept mentioning things like post-traumatic stress disorder, permanent brain damage, and things that people would not disclose for security reasons. On the other hand, Joseph kept telling Kevin how well Sophia was doing without him. Overtly, Joseph's visits were friendly, selfless visits to encourage his colleague's fiancée. Nevertheless, Bernard became a bit suspicious.

> One day he told Sophia, "This guy is too nice. I don't trust him. I don't like the way he looks at you. Why is he inviting you to movies? Be careful!"

As usual Sophia ignored everyone. It was a Wednesday evening, so Bernard and Bertha decided to stop and pray in the nearby church. Joseph came over. He brought her flowers. He started telling her how beautiful she was, and that Kevin was becoming dependent on drugs. When he told her, for the first time, how strong his own feelings for her were, Sophia took his flowers, put them in his vest pocket, dumped the water on his head and told him not to set foot in her house again. When Bernard asked her about Joseph's whereabouts, Sophia quipped with a straight face, "I have no idea, Dad." End of that story.

Kevin kept getting better. A new YouTube video showed him just after the casts were removed from his right arm and leg. He went for intensive rehab and was getting better quicker than expected. The only thing Sophia could note was he had become short-tempered and had difficulty expressing himself. Finally, it was spring, nearly a year since Kevin's deployment. The flowers were blossoming, the leaves were coming back, the birds began singing, and on March twenty-second, Kevin called Sophia.

"Hey baby! Guess what?"

"You are coming home soon?"

"Even better. They have reviewed my records and my service. I am getting an honorable discharge, along with decorations and full pension after a promotion."

"When is this going to happen? Asked Sophia.

"Most likely this summer."

"This summer! You mean three to six months of additional waiting? I think I am coming to see you before then. Tomorrow I am going to see my congressman to see what can be done."

"Remember babe, we are not yet legally married. This is not going to be easy," said Kevin.

"You'll see, Kevin, you'll see."

After talking to Kevin, Sophia went to tell her parents the news. Bertha said immediately, "So, Sophia, why don't you guys get married in October, around his birthday, the way you planned for last year?"

"Mother, do you think I can wait that long?"

"Wait for what? If you mean what I think you mean, then go to City Hall first."

"That's not the same thing." replied Sophia.

"Anyway, if you are thinking like I am thinking, after a year of separation, only City Hall can save you," replied Bertha.

"Do you guys want me to leave the room?" asked Bernard

"Don't be silly," replied Bertha.

"Dad, what is your view about getting married at City Hall?"

"You want my view, or the Biblical view, or our church's view?

"Dad, don't complicate things. What do you—as a human being—think?"

"I believe marriage is a social event. You can get your license from City Hall; the rest is up to you."

Bertha did not say one word.

"I never saw it that way. It is true. But I did not expect that to come of my father's mouth. How *in-ter-es-ting*!"

Sophia left it at that and went to her room.

"What a roller coaster ride this girl has put us on for the last few months!" exclaimed Bernard while helping his wife prepare the soil for some serious spring gardening.

"You can say that again! Still, I am very pleased that she seems to be getting through it all. I thought our lives were tumultuous, but nothing like this."

"In all fairness, we have been there for her. In our times, we went through it all alone. You may have forgotten, but we had some really rough times. I believe the Almighty saved us, despite ourselves, from much trouble."

"Bernard, have you heard the latest?"

"No! Fill me in!"

"Well, Junior seems to have a new girlfriend."

"You're on your own with that one. I can't handle two tsunamis at the same time."

As they were getting ready to go back in, thunder and rain suddenly started. Shortly after, Sophia came home. Junior begged her for her car.

"Why?" asked Sophia.

"I have to meet a sophisticated girl. I need to make a good first impression."

"Junior, why don't you work on your real first impression? Be disciplined; get a real job instead of that Internet sales business of yours. Do something, get a master's—"

"Listen, are you going to lend me the car or not?"

Sophia gave him the key and said, "I know how much gas is in it and how much mileage I have on it. Drive carefully."

Sitting in the living room, Sophia set the official wedding date, the afternoon of October first. If all hurdles were overcome, Kevin should be back by July or mid-August. By then he would have completely recuperated.

"This means we have less than six months to prepare for the wedding. The only way this is possible is to delegate tasks," said Bertha

"Mom, I have it all figured out: Nicole will make the cake—"

"Who is Nicole?" asked Bertha.

"Don't you know Kevin's mother's name by now?" replied Bernard in a teasing tone.

"Lakisha will be the maid of honor. Mom, you make the arrangements for the announcements. Dad, you prepare the wording for the invitation. Mom and I will prepare the guest list. I need a budget where nothing is left out, including the reception hall and the honeymoon. I need a small private and quiet wedding."

"No way! I want a big wedding for my only daughter. I want a wedding that people will talk about for a long time. Something that is bigger and better than Mr. Bernstein's daughter's wedding."

"Mom, you forget two things. Dad is not the mayor like Mr. Bernstein. Second, why be foolish? Give me the money; let me use it as a down payment for our own home or for college tuition for my kids. I have seen people throw big weddings, and then they are still paying the wedding bills while the couple is divorced. What kind of foolishness is that?"

"Honey, am I in charge of the wedding or not?" asked Bertha matter-of-factly.

"Mom, I think Kevin and his mother should have a say in this too. We need to decide where to have the religious ceremony and by whom, where to go for honeymoon, for how long—"

"Well, I believe these months should be spent weighing the reasons why the two of you want to get married and how you are going to stay married." said Bernard.

"I know. I just need to follow your example."

"No!" exclaimed Bernard.

"Why not?"

"You are not Bertha and Kevin is not I. Every couple has a different dynamic between them and must find their own way to adjust and survive. Furthermore, times have changed. Even the concept of marriage has been eroded somewhat. When your mother and I got into such a covenant, we knew we were in it for life. Nowadays, people get married thinking they can always get out of it. I even read about happily married people fantasizing about a divorce; some even advocate a five-year, ten-year marriage contract, renewable only upon mutual request."

Bertha added, "The engagement time is critical to think things through and have a perspective on where you want to take that relationship. Kevin being absent for so long…when he comes back, that will automatically require a period of readjustment. You will notice some changes in him. He will notice some in you."

"After so many traumas, with post-traumatic stress disorder, how is he going to behave? You want to take some serious time to see how the two of you can make it."

"Dad, you mean to tell me that you and Mom were absolutely sure about each other?"

"No. We were absolutely willing to adjust, correct, and agree to disagree with civility, to deal in good faith and remain truthful to each other. We were willing to do everything under the sun in our power to make it work."

"I hear you disagreeing all the time."

"Yes, darling, but we are not disagreeable. We rely on a higher power. We remain committed to the marriage covenant that is bigger than your Dad and me. Anytime a problem comes up, one of us raises the red flag and demands an explanation."

"I guess mom raises the red flag more often than you, Dad."

Bernard said, "I have no comment. It does not really matter who does what. It is important to remain committed. Anyway, this is the time to be clear on what kind of family you are going to have. What church, if any, you are going to attend? Where do you plan to live? How many kids you plan to have? What is your sexual approach? Does anything go? Do you believe in birth control and the use of condoms? Who is going to work and who is going to stay home with the children? Public school, home school, or private school? What do you believe in terms of home sharing activities: washing dishes, taking care of the kids, bills payment, financial responsibilities, savings, and expenses? How are you guys going to cope with your increased sexual appetite when the two of you get back together? You need to have an open discussion on all of these issues and not assume anything. If you have skeletons in your closet that may come out and hurt your relationship with your mate, you must level with him. For example, if someone has a child, a mistress, or is sexually incompetent, this should be explored. However, some past youthful indiscretion that has no bearing in the new relationship should be left alone."

"Do you care to give a few examples, Bernard?" interrupted Bertha.

"Well, for instance, what does anyone have to gain, to show a portfolio of previous relationships when those people involved have gone their separate merry ways. Of course if you get a sexually transmitted disease, or even HIV, you should be fair enough to inform the partner. Because, sooner or later he or she will find out and you will lose each other's trust for a long time. It pays to tell the truth that is so crucially needed to keep the love relationship going."

Bertha added, "This also brings up the issue nowadays to have a full medical evaluation and some mutually agreed upon testing. Furthermore, being engaged does not mean you are married, and stuck at any cost. If you discover that the marriage is going to make you miserable, or even threaten your life physically or mentally, you should never feel it is too late to pull out."

After a long pause, Sophia blurted out, "I wonder if I am ready for this big step in my life."

Bertha replied: "Of course, honey. Don't be silly. You will be just fine. You see, It is like learning how to—you read about it, you learn about it, and you practice. Then when you get to drive, the basic skills are there, they are part of you, and things become natural."

Bernard added, "I was going to give you the ten commandments for a great marriage and the ten things that can kill your marriage. I guess I will save them for another time."

"I agree with you, Dad."

19

Kevin and Sophia's relationship was fairly tumultuous. Many observers and even family members had some serious doubts concerning its future. But somehow they managed to keep their heads above water. Kevin came back and went through some adjustment periods. Finally, the date, October first, arrived.

The night before the wedding, almost everybody was unable to sleep. Sophia found it to be the longest night of her life, counting almost every single hour of the night. Around five in the morning, the phone rang. It was Kevin, who had an exciting idea:

"Hey Sophia, why can't we elope?"

"I have a better idea; there is so much to do in so little time, why don't you come and let's team up to get things done quickly?"

"Well, you know what they say; it is bad luck for the two people who are getting married to see each other just before the wedding."

"I don't believe in luck. Let's not be superstitious. Come over and let's take control."

Kevin joined Sophia and together they went back and forth, here and there, running errands. That is, until Kevin locked the car keys inside the car while it was running, and with Sophia's things in the backseat.

Panic took over, and they yelled, banged, pushed, and pulled: nothing worked. Finally, Kevin broke part of the back window to have access to the car. That was enough to convince them to go their separate ways until the wedding.

20

It was a gorgeous, balmy Sunday; nature was on its best behavior. Beneath a cloudless sky the long awaited dream of both Sophia and Kevin was about to take place. Bertha had had her way about the size of the wedding. One hundred guests watched the sweet and loving couple celebrate their nuptials on a sandy white beach while the breeze gently caressed their faces as they looked into each other's eyes. After a half-hour ceremony, the *I do's* were sealed with a tender kiss. The reception followed at the Ocean View Restaurant (where the ceremony would have been held indoors if the weather had not cooperated). The place was exquisite, with its marble lobby, crystal chandeliers, cathedral ceilings, and oversized windows overlooking the beach. Hors d'oeuvres were passed during the cocktail hour. Dinner was delicious and elegant. The three-tier wedding cake was a work of art. A live orchestra played dinner music and later dance music for the guests.

From the reception to the dress, no detail was too small and no request unattainable. The bride wore an Oscar de la Renta gown that flattered her silhouette; it was lavishly embellished with opulent hand beading and was embroidered with lace appliqué on the finest silk fabric. She was a vision of classic style and beauty. Her bridal bouquet was sophisticated and timeless, with pink roses bound by slivers of lily grass that complemented the six bridesmaids and groomsmen.

The night was memorable. Guests laughed and cried tears of joy. Bernard and his wife were overjoyed and extremely proud. These blissful memories are one they would hold on to forever.

Following Bernard's advice, Sophia and Kevin booked two nights at the Marriott Marquis, a few miles away. The wedding ended late that Sunday but they managed to arrive at the hotel that night. Exhausted and thankful that she survived that night, Sophia figured they would both collapse in each other's arms and consummate their union in the morning. Nonsense thought Kevin. He's been waiting for this moment and dreaming about this night for too long. So he carried her in the bedroom and placed her gently on the king-sized bed, where he began to undress her slowly, layer by layer, until all mysteries were finally revealed. There in all her splendor, chills overtook her body as she was so nervous. He gave her a soft, long kiss, then stared into her eyes and said "Baby, no more excuses! Tonight I'm going to enjoy you." He ran his fingers through her hair, than her neck and down her entire back; he nibbled on her ear and whispered sweet nothings. The sensations shot from her head to her toes. As he journeyed south, he explored every inch of her trembling body, caressing every curve while planting soft wet kisses here and there. While holding him, her eyes tightly closed, she could hardly keep still in the heat of the moment. He was gentle, staying at a slow and steady pace all the while asking if she was okay. The sweet sound of her moans made him want to savor the moment, and he wished it would never end. He made love to her with his mind, body and soul, and she surrendered herself totally. He had delighted, beguiled, and thrilled her to the point of extreme ecstasy. She felt safe and protected in the arms of the man who loved her unconditionally, and she was determined not to disappoint him.

21

The new couple decided to settle in Virginia. Sophia liked the lovely gardens and the beautiful old homes, with historic landmarks and sandy beaches within reasonable driving distance. Kevin liked the mountains and the raceway. Together they felt they could raise a family there while being a few hours away from Sophia's parents. They were happy to share each other's company without separation or others' interference. Kevin got an office job in a nearby government facility, and Sophia found a job as a paralegal in a local law firm. And life went on as they adjusted to married life. They were happy to be together and share their lives: lovely evenings, romantic diners, exchange of surprises, exciting weekends here and there. It was a picture that many could envy and few can truly describe.

They were convinced that such a great life could last forever. They were determined to improve it daily. When love reigns, everything becomes bearable. The couple was swimming in the river of love, basking in happiness, living for each other, and complementing each other. Parents, friends, neighbors, and visitors enjoyed seeing them glowing in love, with the awe of fulfillment surrounding them.

Sophia stayed late in bed regularly on Sunday morning while Kevin would become restless after six a.m.; therefore he usually got up and went for his weekend newspaper.

Kevin enjoyed the privilege of preparing Sophia's breakfast and bringing it to her while she was still in bed. They liked to reward each other with romantic surprises that only young, healthy couples in love can dream of. That Sunday morning, as usual, Kevin prepared breakfast, including Sophia's favorites, and brought it to her with all the sweet nothings that came along. But Sophia was a bit distant, somnolent, and tired. Kevin urged her to eat. She hardly took a few bites. Shortly after, she threw up. She spent the day moody, feeling dizzy, and she stayed in bed most of the time. She told Kevin to be careful, she might be coming down with the flu. After a few days with similar symptoms, and repeated vomiting, and because of Kevin's insistence, she saw her doctor. She returned home with her face beaming with joy and pride. Kevin guessed right: Sophia was pregnant, with all the accompanying signs: irritable moods, morning sickness, malaise, fatigue—Kevin was elated. He never felt so good in his entire life. The couple celebrated such good news by taking a week off just to stay home, relax, and plan for that big change that was coming in their lives. The news spread fast. Parents were becoming grandparents, lovers were becoming parents. It was joy, joy, and joy!

Upon returning back to work, Kevin started noticing changes in the work environment. He was transferred to another department; some people had to quit because of the mishandling of some delicate situations. The entire place was under scrutiny, with the naming of a special commission to look further into that matter. Kevin was getting a lot of pressure at work. Then it did not take long for the pressure at work to be taken home. Slowly but surely, Kevin and Sophia started to put their guard down; their true colors were showing. The daily exigencies of life were taking their toll on them. They had less time to spend with each other, and tension was getting high. During Sophia's first pregnancy, she became so sick she had to take a leave of absence from work. This increased the financial challenges for the family. After staying home alone all day, Sophia could not wait for her husband to come home for some great conversation. Yet, after talking all day at work, and being tired, Kevin was looking forward to come home, enjoy some home cooking, and rest. Life began to change. Things started to seem boring. Remarks they used to laugh at became insults. Kevin's job involved dealing with top secret information for national security. He could not discuss what he was doing. He would call and not be able to talk much or reveal where he was or what he was doing. Sophia became suspicious, crying unexpectedly. Kevin could not take too many days off from the new job. One evening, Kevin called to say that something came up at work; he was not going to be home. That was one of the events that really shook their marriage. In fact, after hanging up on Kevin and calling him irresponsible for leaving a pregnant wife alone at home while he was having fun at work, both of them were really upset. Kevin could not understand the big deal about his inability to go home because of national security duties and resented the expression, *having fun at work*. Sophia, on the other hand, felt Kevin did not give her the time and attention she deserved as a *pregnant wife*. That night Sophia took the train, then a taxi, to go to her parents' home in New York. Upon arriving, she knocked at their door. Bertha opened and was surprised to see her daughter; and so was Bernard. But after some civilities, after details were provided, Bernard made it clear to Sophia that she had made a mistake; her home was now in Virginia. She rested a little and then her parents drove her back home to Virginia to be with her husband.

Luckily, they got home before Kevin had the chance to set foot into the house.

It was a cold day in February with some light snow. Kevin rushed into his home and was surprised to see his in-laws there.

"Hello Mr. and Mrs. Marcel. How nice to see you here—quite unexpectedly!"

"The pleasure is ours," replied Bernard. "We wanted to see how you guys were coping."

Kevin said, "We are coming along fine, aren't we Sophia?"

Sophia gave no answer.

Bertha said "We are not staying; we have quite a few things to take care of back home."

Bernard quickly added, "But before we leave, we just want to emphasize a few things, if we may."

"By all means, please do!" said Kevin.

Everybody got comfortable, including Kevin. Bernard began:

"We are not going to stay and we do not plan to drop in like this either. Now that you have been married for several months, and you are even expecting a baby, we can say you are blessed. We hate to be the bearer of bad news, but we want to emphasize that you are at one of the most vulnerable moments of your marriage. The honeymoon is tapering off; you are facing more and more unexpected challenges daily that are stretching your nerves. This will take a toll on your relationship; it tends to also have its impact psychologically. This is why I personally do not believe in setting a long time for a honeymoon. When you come back you feel strange, and life with all its features is waiting for you. From the first day of your return to real life you are playing catch-up until separation or death. I strongly advocate a day-to-day honeymoon based on finances, availability, type of work, and necessity."

Bertha interrupted, "But the real point that needs to be made is the fact that now is the time when you face the realities of life. You may even feel disappointed. Don't panic. You need time to settle down, to adjust to each other, and to learn the survival tactics for your marriage to last. I am sure you have had some surprises about each other already. There will be even more, because no human being truly knows himself without facing various challenges and temptations. But again, do not panic!"

Bernard continued: "Upon getting married—even before that—there are certain urgent things that need to be discussed:

1. Set the boundaries as to what is expected, what is acceptable, and what your responsibilities are. For example, my friend Jeanine told me that on her wedding night she discovered her husband teasing her by pinching her or throwing the pillow at her, calling her clumsy, and even raising his voice just because she inadvertently spilled some juice on the bed. She immediately set him straight and told him not to play such childish game. She would not tolerate being threatened, put down, or being beaten or yelled at. She was very clear and firm, but tactful. She was not sure of what he was doing, but she would not take any chance to find out. She stopped him right there and then.

2. Beware of at least seven key issues that cause squabbles between married couples.

   a. *Finance:* money management and debt avoidance. Make sure you have a budget, you know how much money comes in, control your expenses, and never fail to save. Ideally, when two people work, they should try to live on one check and save the other one. But because things are so unpredictable, each one should have his or her account based on the arrangement and the type of marriage they have. Avoid debt as much as possible, including credit cards. If one credit card is needed, it should be used when it is required and when the money to pay it in full is already there to pay the bill once it comes. Do not borrow money from your appreciable asset to buy things that are quickly depreciable.

   b. *Philosophy and approach to life:* what do you want in life? Where do you see yourself in six months, one, two, three, and five years from now? What about your partner? What mechanism is used to come to a common decision for the couple and their children?

   c. *Management of day-to-day activities:* there are routine day-to-day exigencies of everyone's existence. Living together should not make it an unfair burden for one partner while the other is vacationing constantly. The house is not a hotel; most people do not have maids, cooks, gardeners, and chauffeurs. Therefore, common sense and basic decency dictate that everyone does his fair share in every aspect of life: cleaning, cooking, various activities while raising kids, etc. Do not lose your cool, and do not disrespect each other. If it is easier for you, assign responsibilities, but be flexible.

d. *Character, habits:* once married, you need some adjustment time. A willingness to improve the condition is paramount. Do not be stubborn and fixed in your own ways. Make an effort to hear and consider the other partner's viewpoint. Take time to develop some new habits together. After a few months the relationship will be stronger: praying together, going to dinner together every Friday night, or going for a walk in the evening or early in the morning are a few examples.

e. *Intimacies:* Sex is a part of intimacy, but it is not the whole picture. You need the proper environment, predisposition, disposition, availability, desire, and ability to perform. Sex should be enjoyable and mutually acceptable. Learn to make an effort to please the other partner. Do not have a fixed idea, do not embargo sex, and do not use it as a means of punishment. Be willing to learn, eager to please, and confident enough to talk about it for a better relationship.

f. *Treatment in public and in private:* the partner wants to be acknowledged, especially in public. Do not fail to introduce him or her to others with warmth and respect.

9. *Communication:* learn to express yourself in good times as well as in bad times. Be quick to congratulate, acknowledge good deeds, be thankful for all minute services rendered, yet be tactful and learn how to express dissatisfaction gracefully. For example: *You are always late* and *You never remember anything* are examples of negative communication. Instead, you could say *I appreciate when you come on time*, or *I thank you for remembering to do this*. Positive reinforcement should be the goal. Do not expect your partner to read your mind or anticipate your needs. Please express yourself without ambiguity, without being sarcastic, disrespectful, or angry. No one is always bad and wrong. Focus on the good things a little more."

Bertha could not wait. So she interjected and said, "Beware of habits that irritate or can slowly eat away at your marriage: boredom and routine; dropping dirty clothes, socks, and sneakers all over; overuse or inappropriate time for TV and phone conversations; keeping the house tidy—Be careful, do not take your relationship for granted; look for ways to spice it up."

Kevin and Sophia looked at each other a bit amused.

Bernard added, "As your parents, we do not want to interfere in your lives. But if you need any advice, both of you should feel free to call me or Bertha for any questions. We will do our best to help whenever we can. We believe that Nicole feels the same way. We do not anticipate serious problems, but if you do face serious challenges, I believe the two of you will seek professional help to avoid disasters."

Bertha added, "If your love and commitment to being together is strong enough, you can face any challenges, including the unknown in the different aspects of your life as a couple."

Bertha and Bernard left the new couple to return home without going over the details of their differences. Afterward, Sophia and Kevin tried to remember some of the advice while ironing out the difficulties in their relationship.

22

Sophia and Kevin managed to live their lives and to learn how to solve their problems as they came. As expected, the first year was really a bumpy and tumultuous road. Sophia gave birth to two children within twenty months: a lovely baby girl and a charming boy. Both were adorable and brought immense joy to their parents and their grandparents. After years of living together, the question was: has the other partner changed or have they learned to adjust and to tolerate or to change each other? They polished each other more and more and seemed to be very happy. Their love grew slowly and through stages. If it began with outside appearance and emotion, it grew through appreciation of inner beauty, a disinterested kind of love that sought the interest of the other first and foremost. If their love started with a sentiment, a mere attraction, it matured through reasoning, maturity, patience, and perseverance. The truth about marriage is it requires both parties to make it work. They must be willing to constantly face the challenges while looking in the same direction. Sophia and Kevin seemed to have found the groove.

While Kevin was out of town on one of his job-related trips, Bertha decided to pay a visit to her daughter and her grandchildren. All four of them had a great time together. At night, while the kids were sleeping, Bertha and Sophia took the time to talk about various subjects.

"Isn't life strange? Years ago, if anyone told me that the two of us could ever sit down and have a civilized conversation, I would have told him that was impossible!" Bertha said.

"There is a time for everything, Mother."

"Tell me something. Are you happy?"

"Yes, Mom, I am quite happy. But I am not sure Kevin is."

"You know men, they are bizarre creatures. We do not always know how to please them. You just have to do your best."

"And they say we are mysterious; they do not know what they are talking about."

"You can say that again!" Bertha replied.

"For instance, for our fifth anniversary, I told him we should go on a vacation. We have not been on one in a while. All he did was shrug his shoulders. Now, Mom, what is that supposed to mean?"

"Sophia, my dear, you remember people keep saying that men and women are different? Such a difference manifests itself in areas you would not believe!"

"So Mom, you are trying to tell me, men are different from women even when it comes to vacations?"

"Yes, indeed, my dear! Remember last time you went on vacation—a year and a half ago? What did you do? You had two little kids to handle in a different environment; how much fun could the two of you have had?"

"But the kids seemed to love it."

"Precisely! You have worked hard. You deserve a break. Vacation is always welcome. But what does vacation mean to you? Its definition varies with age, time and circumstances. Overall, most men see vacation as a semi-honeymoon.

For a man to have a good vacation with his spouse, he wants:

- Time alone with his wife and a lot of intimacy—this includes repeated sexual sessions, and he wishes he could repeat his honeymoon performance or even better, because he feels he has more experience.

- Time alone for himself so he can intermingle with friends or meet new people, read, or participate in sports. No nagging, no heavy schedule, no worries about the upcoming bills. It is not the time for criticism.

- Idle time just to be himself again, to unwind and relax without anybody bossing him around.

- Time with his soulmate should be pleasant, playful, appreciative, and positive. It is a refueling session, a renewal experience to count blessings, think about the great privilege to be in each other's lives, and to engage in the course of life together with the same vision.

For the woman, vacation is a time for great adventure, to have fun and lay back. The expectations include:

- The ability to have someone to drive her anywhere and everywhere she wants at any time. She intends to enjoy her vacation. She is not likely to be physically tired when going on vacation and gets her money's worth in using whatever is available and is part of the package.

- The ability to go shopping almost every day of the vacation.

- The ability to go out to eat and not have to cook.

- The ability to go swimming whenever she wants to or to participate in any other activities that she likes.

Sex is the icing on the cake, while it is the main course for most men."

"I can tell you, last vacation, Kevin was awful. He was irritable and lazy. All he wanted to do was stay in bed and watch TV. I told him we could do that at home."

"He was on vacation. You were likely so busy with the kids, you paid him little attention. He had high expectations. Now that you are again talking about a vacation, he is wondering whether or not he is willing to go drive people around and be bossed around, with little of what he wants. He figures he is better off working and getting paid for it."

"So how do we reconcile these two approaches?"

Bertha replied quickly:

1. "Be flexible and considerate (this means that each partner needs to be sensitive to the other's favorites. If only one has to compromise all the time, sooner or later, the other one may explode).

2. Plan the vacation together, early enough to make reservations and other necessary major arrangements.

3. Be realistic, and have a feasible budget with a margin of fifteen to twenty-five percent extra for emergencies.

4. Give your partner some freedom, and treat him or her as a responsible adult. Allow time to indulge and unwind and space to breathe—to decide what to wear, what to do, where to sit, what to eat (even if it's not all that healthy). One meal on vacation is not likely to be your partner's tombstone unless it is a life-threatening issue. Remember that you are both on vacation!"

"Believe me Mom, you make me even more confused!"

"Why?"

"We are not 'just people', we are his family, his wife and his children."

"He knows that. Believe me he cares about you guys. But let's face it, he needs some refueling. He needs some time alone with you. Right now he may be fighting against the idea that he is stuck forever. For a young man in this day and age, this is scary, especially if he works with guys who are real players. He is looking back and is wondering what happened to the woman who was always ready to go places and have fun. Of course this is not always possible. Nevertheless, from time to time, at least show him and give him a good time, challenge him, surprise him, and keep the romance going. Avoid a routine love life. Otherwise it becomes lame and boring, and he may start to look around. You need a good time yourself, don't you? The nurturing tendency in you makes you love and care for your two adorable, healthy children. Already you are looking forward to sharing their activities: piano or flute lessons, tennis, or swimming, or ballet—But do not neglect the other aspects of life. You need to keep your man, so show some excitement!"

"I thought you would be on my side, Mom. This guy got me pregnant twice, almost back to back. It could have even been more. It is his fault that things are the way they are. So what do you suggest?"

"Find time for the two of you. You must build up an ever-present romantic relationship. Simple things such as: calling your partner daily while at work and writing him love notes. Have a 'couple diary' where each tries to outdo the other in romantic, spicy compliments and exciting comments; be genuine, be flexible, and improvise surprising spots in the house to make love; leave spare time for massages; arrange for surprising dates and rendezvous; tease him about what you reserve for him once in a while; and use your imagination. After a dinner, be his dessert with ice cream, leave a surprising note on his windshield signed by a secret admirer, and tell him how happy and fortunate you are to have him, learn to make any occasion or holiday, a great one to celebrate with him. Take him to a movie, a game, a concert, or a show; write him emails and send him text messages. Don't forget to congratulate him after a great moment, be spontaneous, and learn to fool around in improvised ways and places—"

"So mother, what about him? What does he do?"

"Focus on what you can do. Shower him with love and pleasant surprise. Believe me; he will at least try to meet your challenges. The fact of the matter is, what I am telling you should be valid for the two of you. It is not for one person to do the giving, and the other to just receive. No! For instance, he can send you flowers at work, he can take you to work and then pick you up for a surprise party, make you breakfast in bed on weekends, you can attend conferences together, get a babysitter every now and then for the two of you to go on a romantic date somewhere, shower together once in a while, and keep flirting with each other. Use your wild imagination; the scenarios and events will be limitless and you will grow old together, while doing your best to stay attractive and spoil each other without being a burden or a bore. Start early, and develop good habits. Otherwise, bills, bills, and more bills added to life's frustrations and deceptions will eat you alive; and there will be nothing but a lame, dark, and stressful life. This is what can destroy your family at any stage of your lives. You do not want to become two partners arguing about the bills, the babysitter, and school…"

"Mom, where did you learn all these things? When I look at you and Dad, you look like two saints. I can't believe you guys could be doing these kinds of things."

"Believe me, honey, life is a school with an open book. But the book is so voluminous, you must put to use immediately every lesson you learn; otherwise you may not find the chapter in time when you need it. When you find a partner to your liking these days, you must fight to keep him. Good people are hard to come by. Anyway, to make a long story short, if the two of you want a short vacation alone, maybe something can be arranged. Maybe some family members, some parents can help. Remember, a man is constantly thinking about intimacy; don't disappoint him, and don't be boring. Show him that tiger that all of us have inside of us when we want to challenge them; otherwise, he will start looking, even fantasizing. We must do our best."

Sophia smiled. She understood the disguised offer but had to interrupt the dialogue to attend to her daughter, who had just woken up and started crying.

23

Thanksgiving Day is a great moment for family members to gather together and reminisce. It is a time to pause and reflect, to be grateful for all the blessings in life, to eat and to share a good time. Bernard and Bertha were particularly looking forward to this fourth Thursday of every November. Bertha knew she would have the privilege of spending time with her grandchildren. Sophia was planning to get there a bit earlier than Kevin to help her mother prepare the meal. The menu was decided: smoked turkey, green bean casserole, sweet potatoes, pumpkin pie, mashed potatoes, stuffing, cabernet cranberry sauce, and sugar-free apple pie for Dad, cheddar cheese, Mom's favorite coconut cream pie, raspberry white chocolate cake—It was going to be a big dinner and people were likely to eat leftovers until Christmas. Sophia and Bertha talked about it to the point that Bernard's mouth was already salivating and he began to smell the aroma from anticipation.

One week prior to the great event, Bertha received a frantic call from Sophia.

> "Mom, I have had it! That's it. I am through with Kevin. I want a divorce…"
>
> "Whoa! Slow down, not so fast. Take a deep breath and compose your thoughts. What is going on with the two of you? Wasn't everything perfect last week? What has changed so drastically?"

"No time to talk. That's it. I want him out of my life, out of my children's life."

"So you want a divorce?"

"I am telling you I am leaving him. That's a fact!"

"Sophia, can we talk about it when we meet for Thanksgiving?"

"Mom, you don't get it do you? There won't be any Thanksgiving! Everything is through!"

"Honey, calm down. You still have not told me why."

"Do you really want to know, Mom? I am old enough to make my own decisions—"

"I know that, dear. But you called me, didn't you?"

"Well if you have to know, Kevin is having an affair!"

"What! Are you sure?"

"What do you mean? I am telling you."

"What makes you think so?"

"I do not think so, I know so!"

"Listen, your Dad wants to talk to you."

"I can't talk to him right now. I'll email him. Bye!" Sophia hung up.

Some scattered snowflakes were melting on the streets of New York; everything was the same as usual, and somehow Bertha felt as if everything was frozen around her. She turned to Bernard and declared:

"Are we going to see what is going on?"

"Oh no! Sophia is mature enough to handle the situation. We cannot pop up in her life every time something comes up," replied Bernard.

"Here you go again. We are not talking about every time. They have been married for five years; if they had to call us for everything, you would not have time to sleep."

Bernard said, "Anyway, I believe Sophia should handle her own problems. Furthermore, I suggest we do not call her or take any of her phone calls until next Thursday."

"What? By then if Kevin kills my daughter, I will never forgive you."

"Bertha, my dear, trust me on this one. Sophia can take care of herself. Our phone has an answering machine. We need to teach her a lesson."

"I agree with you and I support the decision, but if she dies, what lesson could she have learned?"

"Believe me," insisted Bernard. "She won't die. Haven't you noticed when she really wants to do something she does it?"

Bertha left Bernard in the living room and went to take care of her daily routine but was unable to concentrate. Instead, all kinds of macabre thoughts kept coming into her mind. The remaining six days left before Thanksgiving were awfully quiet. Bertha, who was usually so extraverted, said almost nothing. On Tuesday, two days before Thanksgiving, Bernard managed to steal the list of all the needed ingredients for Thursday's menu, went out with one of the neighbors, and bought all that was necessary for the dinner.

On Tuesday night, he said, "Hey Bertha, you know, I have been thinking. I have a great idea!"

Bertha acted as if she did not hear. Bernard repeated himself, "Bertha I believe I have a wonderful idea."

"Really!" she quipped casually.

"Why don't we drive to Virginia Wednesday and stay over at Kevin and Sophia's house for Thanksgiving?"

"It sounds great but you and I know Sophia is likely to have decided not to do anything, to ignore the holiday altogether because she is bitter. You said you were not going to call her until Thursday; have you changed your mind?"

"No! Nothing has changed in that domain! We can always bring her what is needed for the feast."

"I have no time for such a crazy plan," replied Bertha. "I can't rush through the market the day before Thanksgiving. It is a madhouse there. I may not even find all that I want, anyway."

"Bertha, Bertha, Bertha, my dear, you worry yourself too much. Trust me!"

"Well with your smart idea, how would you deal with the fact she may decide to come to see us here? So you go there, she comes here. How amusingly stupid and awkward would that be?"

"This is easy. I already know that Kevin is working all day Wednesday. Sophia is not likely to drive with the kids alone. So, just before we leave, I will call her from my unlisted cell phone. She will not answer. (She never answers restricted numbers.) We will leave a message that we won't be here Thursday, and that we have other plans. Then we will not answer the phone when she calls."

Bertha gave one of her big smiles and agreed passively, but she was not fully convinced. Besides, she liked to see things well planned. By midday Wednesday, Bernard and Bertha were on their way to see their daughter. Bertha was delighted to see that Bernard had already bought all that was necessary for Thanksgiving dinner. She was quite pleased, except for the eggnog and the butter that was melting on the seat because Bernard did not want to risk raising any suspicion by taking them inside the house.

The six-hour trip took almost eight hours because of heavy traffic. Bernard and Bertha made the best out of it by stopping at the outlet stores and doing some shopping. Bertha told Bernard how much she loved the fact he was always so resourceful but is sometimes confusing. He tended to brag without saying anything by showing his smug face. Those eight hours also gave them time to think of all the possible scenarios they might find when they arrived. They made the firm decision to play it fair. They would act as if they did not know anything and take a fresh, unbiased look at the situation. Bertha agreed but deep inside was determined to do some detective work herself to decide what that "affair" was all about. They arrived while the Angelus bell was ringing that Wednesday night. Bernard asked Bertha to call first, before ringing the doorbell.

"Hello!" responded Sophia.

"Is this Sophia and Kevin's residence?" Bertha tried to disguise her voice.

"Yes!"

"Can we come in?"

"Who are you?" asked Sophia.

"We are some of Kevin's old friends," answered Bertha, cracking up laughing.

Sophia opened the door. There stood her Mom and Dad. She jumped up and down like a kid, and so did the grandchildren.

Kevin was sleeping but the joyful noise woke him up.

He came out and warmly welcomed them. It was dinnertime, and everybody ate. Bernard and Kevin unloaded the SUV. Then the two of them went for a drive, leaving Sophia and Bertha home with the children.

While father and son-in-law were out, after the kids went to bed, Bertha went right back into the issue that was upsetting her.

"Sophia, sometimes I wonder if you are trying to give me a heart attack. You called me frantically to tell me you are leaving…you are getting a divorce…I thought I was coming to an unknown address and you and kids had been placed in a shelter. But I see you and your family radiant with happiness. What is wrong with you?"

"Mom, when I called you I was very upset. I am still distressed by Kevin's behavior, which is becoming more and more despicable and puzzling."

"Sophia, let's get to the bottom of this; you said over the phone that you think Kevin is having an affair, didn't you? If so, what made you draw such a drastic conclusion?"

"Mom, as I have mentioned to you in the past, Kevin cannot talk to me or anyone about his job. He claims it is top security. Every now and then, he comes home past midnight. He has been fairly distant. Can you believe Kevin has not touched me for three weeks? He gives me all kinds of excuses that are not worth divulging."

"Hold it Sophia. Have you examined the common causes that tamper a man's sexual desires and performance?"

"Come on, Mom! We went over this before. They include physical health and emotional trouble, boredom, the ever presence of children, worries, burdens, anger, depression, stress, anxiety, sexual problems such as erectile dysfunction, increased discomfort, disgust, fears, etc. Believe me, he is fine. He may have discovered a new pastime. I usually could get through to him at work by calling a main number. The other day I called that number, and the lady who has become a bit friendly with me at that number told me, in strict confidence, that Kevin has not been at work for days. Mom, every morning Kevin leaves home well dressed. He has not been to his regular job. When he comes home he is tired; he barely interacts with us here. You tell me what conclusion I am to draw."

"When his job told you he has not been there for days, did you call him on his cell?"

"Yes, I did."

"What did he tell you?"

"I asked him where he was. He told me he was at work."

"Really? Sophia, has he been coming home continuously late during those few days?"

"Not necessarily. Mother, remember I am the one in the legal field here!"

"Sure, but not for yourself. So far all you tell me can be just a coincidence. Maybe the lady who told you that wants to break up your marriage. Could it be she wants him for herself or a friend?"

Sophia exploded with a big sarcastic laugh and said,

"You mean to tell me she wants to derail my marriage? Why? The lady does not even know us. Kevin told me the place is huge and there are many people there. They come, get their assignments, and leave. Some are gone for days, or weeks or even months before they come back. Why would she choose Kevin, mother?"

"I am sure Kevin is talking to your father right now, and I am convinced he has a good explanation for his so-called strange behavior."

"Wait a minute, said Sophia. "Why did she tell me that?"

"Why did who tell you what, Sophia?"

"Why did the lady at the Pentagon tell me that Kevin had been out?

"Listen Sophia, you are reading too much into nothing now. You are getting to be paranoid and going crazy. By the way, I didn't know Kevin was working at the Pentagon."

"Who told you that, mother?"

"You just did, my dear!"

"I did! Oh I am losing my mind. Please forgive me. Do not repeat that to anyone. Kevin would kill me if he ever found out that I told you, yet you just gave me a lead I did not see before. That number is always on his cell phone day and night; he keeps calling that number. Perhaps, it is to talk to her."

"Come on! You mean to tell me that lady lives there? Anytime he calls, she is there? You worry too much Sophia. So who is Kevin working for? What's the big secret? What's the big deal? Is he really working or faking it? What does he do? Please tell me. Do you really know?"

"Mom, forget about everything I told you. Please delete all that from your brain."

"Sophia, this is serious stuff. You do not go around telling a man he is unfaithful unless you have some irrefutable proof. Otherwise you may be giving him ideas. Be careful, my darling."

"I know Mom. I always jump to conclusions."

"Well, it is time to stop now, especially as a lawyer by profession. Let me remind you of a few signs that may raise your suspicion about him being unfaithful: being detached and preoccupied, lack of dialogue, irrational behavior, dumb excuses that can easily be refuted, changes in ways of life (lying, being overly concerned about phone calls, pretending to work while on vacation or sick, and losing interest in the couple's intimacy).

Of course these are signs. Even then, you must also ask yourself: Have there been reasons for your partner to be unfaithful? Here are a few:

1. Boredom, routine, cold, lackluster sexual performances, lack of satisfaction; the partner may be looking for excitement, novelty, adventure, or is seeking to satisfy curiosity.

2. Rigidity, prudery, confusion, and disharmony between partners. One has a liberal viewpoint, the other is very conservative. The key is to be mutually enjoyable and agreeable.

3. Nostalgia for youth, midlife crisis, the desire to prove oneself, or fight self-doubt. Partners need to encourage and appreciate each other and be understanding and mindful of communications and coded messages that may be misinterpreted.

4. Perceiving sex as a duty, rather than another way to express love, fulfill desires, relax, and enjoy each other. The partners need to create the proper

setting to make each other feel comfortable. If there are unresolved issues, resentment, nonsexual cares, or if people are querulous, negative, and jealous, then the passion is killed before bedtime.

5. In the case of broken trust, disappointment, abuse, and neglect, one may fail to weigh all the consequences of behavior and destroy all the positive capital invested in married life.

6. Of course, we must be aware of emotional affairs, and financial infidelity; some people are sick, they have high libido and are always craving sex. These people need to have their problems addressed by professionals.

Sophia, even if you forget everything else, listen carefully to what I am about to say: the decision to divorce should be the last thing on your mind. You need to grasp the reality of the situation, gather all the pertinent facts, and have irrefutable proof, not hunches, deductions, emotion, or appearances. Then consider the options and their consequences. Always look into the lives of those who want you to throw in the towel. Know who your counselors are and what their hidden motives are. Never rush into a conclusion; take your time. All in all, divorce is usually not the best decision, especially when you have children involved. Of course, no one would ask you to stay in a situation where you may have to pay with your life. But be careful and do not rush into anything. Never ignore the fact that all families have conflicts. The key is how they approach them."

Before Bertha could add one more word, Bernard and Kevin walked in. They joined the ladies in the basement, and sat down. Everything became quiet for a while.

Bertha broke the silence and asked, "So, what did you guys talk about?"

Kevin and Bernard looked at each other, not knowing what to say. Bernard spoke up. "We talked man to man about routine things, nothing special."

"Yes, we had a man to man dialogue," added Kevin, who seemed more relaxed.

Bertha said, "Give me a break guys. You mean to tell me you spent the time talking about what teams will make it to the Super bowl this year, while Sophia and I were here talking about the latest outfits in Vogue. I wasn't born yesterday."

Bernard tried to change the subject. He said, "What smells so good, Sophia?"

Bertha answered, "Thanksgiving preparations for tomorrow. Don't even think about it yet!"

Bernard replied, "Oh yeah! Well, it is getting late and I think Kevin and Sophia need to talk. Bertha, let's go to our room."

"All of us can chit-chat; there is nothing special that Kevin and I have to talk about now that would require seclusion and privacy. Right Kevin?" Sophia made a face.

"I think you are right, Sophia." said Kevin.

"Are you sure, Kev?" asked Bernard.

"Yes, I am sure."

"So let's sit and talk. I am all ears!" exclaimed Bertha.

"But we are already sitting, Bertha!" said Bernard teasingly.

"Never mind! You know what I mean." replied Bertha

who quickly turned to Kevin and asked, "So, Kev, what would you like to talk about, besides sports and politics? Pretend I am not here."

Everybody laughed at Bertha, because they knew it was impossible for Bertha to not say a word while others were talking. Bertha knew it, too.

Kevin cleared his throat and began, while gazing at no one in particular, "First of all, I want to thank my in-laws for this opportune visit. All things work together well. I am sure all of us here are grateful and happy to see them, especially Brenda and Marvin. For the last few days, I have not been myself. I suppose Sophia has been upset about the whole thing. That makes the situation even worse and more tense here at home. But now I think everything is under control. We want peace and love as usual in this house, right honey?"

Sophia replied: "I don't know what you are talking about, Kevin. First of all, your bizarre behavior has been going on for weeks, not days. Second of all, do not assume you know why I am upset. Third of all, I am not the one to be blamed for making the situation worse. Now, in the baseball game, three strikes you are out, dear."

"I am sure your dad also told you that the same batter can come back to bat—"

"Yes. This time, make sure you hit a home run. Because a single or double won't do."

Everybody laughed, except Sophia. "The woman means business!" interjected Bernard. He continued, "Isn't love strange? You meet someone you hardly know and dedicate your entire existence to him or her. When you love, you care, you worry, you are jealous, you are hungry, you are happy, you are hot, you are cold—so many emotions are bound together in love. Get this, Kev, I still get a kick out of the story when—many years ago—I ran out of cologne, and I started using my wife's. Coincidentally, Bertha began to give me the cold shoulder. I thought nothing of it, because I was always busy anyway. One day, she was going shopping, and she asked me if I wanted anything. I told her to get me some men's cologne because I had been using her perfume. She cracked up laughing and said, 'I thought you were having an affair and that smell came from another woman.' She was so blinded; she could not even identify her own perfume. So go figure."

"You should talk!" exclaimed Bertha. "What about you wanting to move out of our first home because one neighbor—an old man—kept calling me 'dear sweetie' whenever he saw me, which was not very often."

Bernard said, "I was young and foolish then. Anyway, this is not about you and me Bertha. Kevin, I am sorry; do you guys still want us around, or should we vanish?"

"It's okay," replied Kevin.

"So, go ahead and hit that ball out of the park, Kev!" said Bernard.

"I am not a good batter. To put it all into perspective, four months ago I got a new boss at work. For some reason, she and I could never see eye to eye. Everything I do is wrong. Unfortunately, I lost my security badge three times in a few months. She decided that was unacceptable. She revoked my access to some secured areas and required that I go through the entire security process again for clearance. In late September, she gave me an assignment out of town for two weeks that would not only keep me away from home but also make me miss my wedding anniversary. I refused the assignment…"

"You did what?" interrupted Sophia.

"I told her no. I was not doing that."

"So what did she do?" asked Sophia.

"A few days later, I received a letter in which she stated that she had reviewed my record. I have had a lot of sick days, tardiness, and losing secured badges. This made me a bad example for the other employees. I needed to shape up. I was suspended for thirty days without pay. The next warning would be my termination."

"Good heavens! Why didn't you tell me all that, Kevin?" asked Sophia, fuming.

"Well, I did not want to get you worried. You have your own job, and you told me how tough it is as a young female black lawyer to make it in this place. You have the kids. We are running behind on our mortgage. The subprime rate is choking us. We are even struggling to put food on the table. How do you expect me to find the courage to give you such bad news? We are talking about my dignity as a man here. I did not want to add any more to your burdens, let alone embarrass myself."

"What kind of foolishness is this? Don't you realize it is tougher to worry about the unknown than the known? Here I am, my imagination is running wild with all kinds of possibilities to explain your behavior, when a simple candid explanation would have made a world of difference."

"I am sorry Sophia. I blew it; can you forgive me?"

"Wait a minute! What have you been doing—leaving home every day pretending to go to work. I'd love to hear that explanation, too!"

"There is nothing to explain. Every day, I go to Joe's father's shop and I fill in for a few salesmen on their days off and get paid on commission. I had to do something. I could not stay in bed crying or hanging out depressed, watching people pass by or even run the risk of being kicked out of the house."

"It is your call; I believe, in a solid marriage, there needs to be trust and good communication. You keep preaching this to me. But obviously you are not listening to your own sermon, are you?"

"Again, I am sorry."

"So what do you plan to do, Kevin?" asked Sophia.

"Well, Denise kept me up to date. She told me that the lady was transferred. One of my coworkers replaced her. I spoke to the new boss. So I plan to return to work on Monday."

"By the way, who is Denise?" Sophia enquired.

"She is the lady you talked to any time you called me. Do you know that Denise used to be in the same class with my mother in junior high school?"

Bernard and Bertha looked at each other, amused, excused themselves, and went to bed, relieved to know the whole episode was blown out of proportion and was caused by lack of communication and too much pride.

The following day was lovely; Bertha spent her time between the kitchen and the kids, who were enjoying the company of their grandparents. Everyone had a great time together, and dinner was delicious. That weekend was a blessing for all. Bernard thanked God for the received blessing and for those to come. Then Bertha and Bernard returned home to continue their own lives.

24

Married life is full of joy and excitement, but also challenges of all kinds. The key is to stay alert and keep working on ways to improve the couple's relationship. The challenges—the peaks and valleys—give zest to married life and keep it from becoming routine. There is always something going on. It was Christmas morning. Kevin got up early. He shuffled out to get some coffee in the kitchen. Since he was restless, he went down to his office. He turned on the computer. Ensconced in his armchair, listening to some Christmas carols, he was also checking email and answering machine messages. About six o'clock, the phone rang; the number was from out of state. He rushed to pick it up to avoid waking up the other members of the family, who were fast asleep after spending most of the night awake and watching. A nurse from a hospital in Florida was on the other end. Kevin stood up and braced himself for the worst. He learned that his mother arrived at the hospital two nights earlier, unconscious, with no identification and no information. She had had a stroke and had seized three times. They had thought she was not going to make it.

Fortunately, two days later, she was awake and alert; she spoke with slurred speech and had a mild weakness on her left side. She was able to give them her information earlier that same morning. After obtaining the appropriate information, Kevin hung up the phone and remained glued to the chair, not knowing what to say or do. Various ideas were running through his head, but none seemed to make much sense. It was that strange feeling that everyone has about their parents that is odd and hard to describe. Your intellect is telling you that your parents, like every human being, will get old and eventually die. But somehow you ignore that idea; you believe by not even giving it a second thought that you may never have to deal with such a morbid, unpleasant situation. Then one day you get one of those calls or you bump into the reality where Dad or Mom or both are no longer that strong person you want to be with forever. What do you do? Is this that inevitable time? You even want to bargain: not now! I need time to make up with my parents, to show them how much I appreciate them, to beg for forgiveness, or to be reconciled, regardless of who is at fault. But the exigencies of life keep you going, and you never have that precious time to do what you have longed to do with them. As children, so many times we resent our parents for the way they treated us in the past. We feel they were unfair. Then we get older, and we have our own children. We look back and reason: our parents were not that bad after all. On the contrary, they did a good job raising us. As these ideas are going through our minds, we say to ourselves *someday, sometime, we need to do something special to mark our appreciation for our parents*. Alas! time flies and we are so busy making a living on our own, we lose track of time. Then suddenly, the news hits us and we are caught off guard. Kevin was in a similar frame of mind. He saw his childhood pass by in front of him. He thought about his family, his parents, his brother and sister, the good times, the not so great times—and the waves of nostalgia almost overwhelmed him. The situation at work did not allow him to go and see his mother unless it was absolutely necessary. While he was thinking about all the possibilities, Sophia came from behind and began to gently massage his neck. He remained tense and almost motionless. So Sophia said, "What is wrong, honey?"

"Nothing!" replied Kevin with his neck down to his chest.

"Well, last night you were very cheerful. What is going on?"

"I got a call about my mother…"

"What happened? Is she all right?" inquired Sophia, who sat on his lap.

Kevin told her about what he knew. After some serious considerations, they agreed to send Sophia to see Nicole.

Nicole, it turned out, would not be able to live on her own for a while. With the only choice being putting Nicole in a nursing home or bringing her mother-in-law to Virginia, Sophia chose the latter, after informing Kevin that it was only going to be temporary. Sophia and her mother-in-law managed to fly from Florida to Virginia.

In the meantime, Sophia and her parents continued to stay in touch. Upon learning about the presence of Kevin's mother in the house with the children, Bernard sent the following email:

> *My beloved daughter,*
>
> *I really applaud your decision to have Nicole live with you. I know it is a temporary situation. Still, believe me, life in itself is temporary. I know you are aware that living with in-laws is difficult. Be realistic enough to avoid having Kevin choose between you and his mother. Instead, let the two of you face every*

challenge jointly. Let Kevin talk to her regarding what is not acceptable. Lend her your ears for her to vent her frustrations, and be wise enough not to join with her if she ventures into criticizing her son or anyone from her family. Of course her mere presence is going to change the dynamic in the house between you, your husband, and the children. Please remain respectful and polite. Let her know from the start what the structure is in your house. You and Kevin are the ones raising the kids with your values. Your house is kept as you like it. You need privacy with your husband. All in all, with a positive attitude and some mutual understanding, I hope things will remain stable until you and Kevin decide otherwise.

Mom sends you and yours her heartfelt greetings.

Love,

Dad

Initially, Kevin was devastated to see his mother so weak. The transition and the period of adaptation was not easy. Nicole used to be so independent and so full of life. She could not cope with the idea of being physically impaired and dependent upon others for her needs. She went into a bout of withdrawal, staying only in her room, not eating, not even taking care of her hygiene. This was quite atypical for her. She was seen by physicians who diagnosed her with depression and put her on some mood elevators.

Slowly but surely, Nicole got much better, closer to her baseline, but it took her two and a half years to get to the point that her doctors judged her eighty-five percent recovered. She began to help out in the family. She started helping the grandchildren with homework, she babysat, and she did chores around the house. She was really a great help. Then, Sophia started noticing some empty liquor bottles in the trash. She knew that nobody else in the house drank. When Sophia asked her about it, Nicole became very defensive. Instead of answering with yes or no to the question of drinking, she started complaining to her son about the fact that her daughter-in-law did not respect her, asked her questions she should not have, and treated her like a child. Later on she began to get a bit louder, restless, more aggressive, and more intrusive. She started commenting about the way the house was kept, the way the children were raised, the outfits Sophia wore, Kevin's hairstyle, and the food. The cohabitation became quite uncomfortable. One day, Nicole was really drunk, sleeping on the couch with half a bottle of vodka by her side, while the children were watching all kinds of shows on TV. That was enough! Sophia decided not to leave the kids with her anymore. It was three days before Nicole was sober enough for a meaningful talk.

25

For a few months, Sophia and Kevin had not heard from Bernard and Bertha. It seems, as time goes by, people are so engulfed in their busy daily lives they choose silence as their best way of expressing their love. Sophia wondered about that whole business of human existence. You love so many people. You would like to have them all under one roof living together peacefully. However, it is practically impossible. Everyone has to make a living, carrying the love inside, sometimes not even knowing how to express it or prove it. Sophia wished she could change things. Similar thoughts kept bouncing in and out of her mind while she was driving to work. Later that day she went shopping to pick up a few things needed for the house. She ran into her uncle Theo.

"Uncle Theo, Auntie Norma, how are you?" asked Sophia.
"It's been a long time since I've seen you. We'll have to get together soon"

"That's okay," replied Theo. "So Bernard gave us a big scare the other day, didn't he?"

"What? What are you talking about, Uncle Theo?"

"You mean you didn't know that your dad was sick? He is all right now. I went and saw him last week and he is fine. I am sorry. I thought you knew, Sophia."

Sophia became still. "I don't believe this. I saw Dad at my brother's wedding in Chicago two months ago. He was fine. He promised me an email which I never received. That was unusual. I should have guessed that something was wrong." She did not know how much more to say. She thanked Uncle Theo and his wife, and they went their separate ways.

When she got home, the phone rang. Sophia picked it up.

"Hi Mom, how are things?"

"Everything is fine."

"How is Dad? I just ran into Uncle Theo he told me how sick Dad was—"

"Your Dad had a little heart condition. It was not life-threatening. He and I agreed not to tell you, fearing that you would worry too much and that it would disrupt your entire life schedule."

"Mom, that is not a good excuse. Dad could have been dead. Please promise me that nothing like that will be kept away from me in the future."

"Okay, Sophia."

"May I speak to him?"

"Your Dad went out of town; he will be back tomorrow."

"Mom, why didn't you go with him? Is he well enough to travel alone?"

"Yes, my dear. He is okay. Listen Sophia, we need to be practical. All of us go through stages in this life and at each moment we must make the appropriate adjustments. Like you, we were young, we got married, and we had children. Now our children are married. Their progeny go to school, then reach adulthood, and so on and so forth."

"Mom, what are you trying to tell me? You sound very fatalistic. Are you preparing me for some bad news?"

"No honey, I am not. I am being realistic. At this stage in the game, your dad and I are doing what we like and taking things as they come. We are very blessed to see all these stages in life. You need to do better than us. Try to stay out of debt, keep your marriage on solid ground, and pray for your kids to grow up to become decent citizens in the society. That's what life is about! Some people go on to live a long time with illnesses such as Parkinson's, have a stroke or a heart attack, develop dementia, and get in car accidents. A few make it in good health. No one knows the future. Your dad and I are enjoying every single day."

"Mom, is there anything else I need to know?"

"Like what, my dear? What do you mean?"

"Well, like I said, you sound like someone who is preparing me for some bad news."

"Oh no! I just want you to realize we are getting old. Your generation is taking over, and you need to get used to such an idea. It is often challenging for the younger generation to see their parents getting old right under their eyes. But these are the facts of life."

"I'm going to give Dad a call on his cell."

"Okay, do that. Kiss my cuties for me. How is married life?"

"Everything is wonderful, Mother! Bye!"

That became a wake-up call. Sophia realized once again that although love keeps bouncing around, life is so precious and passes by so fast, and no one can ever fully let his love be known, and felt by others for whom they care about very much. The kids were growing up fast. Dad and Mom were getting old. She and Kevin were not spring chickens either. She spoke to her dad before going to bed.

The night went by slowly.

It was a brand new Tuesday morning. Sophia's family woke up early. The weather was not so great. It was cloudy, rainy, windy, and cold, just enough to dampen one's mood. Sophia was asking herself what the purpose of her life on this earth was. But there was no time to answer. The list of tasks was long: children to take to school, clothes to be taken to the cleaners, the car to take to the mechanic's, and then a bus to take to work in the rain. This kept her going and prevented her from too much deep reflection. Fortunately at work, it was a light day. Kevin called and they went to lunch together.

Kevin asked, "What is going on in that great brain of yours? What are you thinking?"

"I think I am going to write a book," replied Sophia with her dark sunglasses on, hiding her watery eyes.

"What would that book be about?" asked Kevin.

"I want to write about life, about what I think is wrong with it…its fragility, its unfairness. Look at us. Why can't we get the most out of it now, do all the things we enjoy now? Then we will work when we are ready to retire from life. Think of it, Kevin—We spend our entire lives chasing material possessions, doing jobs we do not even like. We pretend to be happy when we do not even know what happiness is. Like they say, we are like dogs. We keep chasing our tails, and we get nowhere and then drop dead. Tell me Kevin, is this what life is all about? I have some serious questions I need to ask."

"Babe, what is getting into you? Why worry about the future, sobbing about the past, when we have today, when together we can forge a bright future for us and for our children? I believe there are good things awaiting us. Why not be thankful we are alive and young? Why not capitalize on our energy, our health, and all the positive things that have happened to us?"

"This is my problem with you. I am addressing a serious issue, and here you are sounding like a twelve-step program. Really, tell me Kevin, do you know anyone who has been living, and at the end of their coil can say they had lived a great life?"

"Yes! Your Dad!"

"Kevin, did my father ever tell you himself that he has had a great life?"

"Yes, Sophia. He and I were at a restaurant not too long ago and he told me, among other things—I am just paraphrasing—Kevin, my son, when you are young, you find so many things you want to do. You have so many options. You have so many offers, and there are so many temptations. The best thing for me, as I am getting old now, is to know I have always lived up to my convictions. There were times when I wish I did a few things just out of curiosity. But now I know I have had a great life. I can look anyone straight in the eye. I have nothing to be ashamed of. Some of my friends used to find me boring. Of course all of us have done some foolish things in our youth, but I have done nothing shameful."

"My Dad told you that?"

"Yes, he did."

Sophia jumped up, kissed him and told him, "Thank you for soothing my soul. I feel like I am losing my parents, and I am scared." Kevin and Sophia hugged each other.

Kevin told her, "I am still expecting your bestseller."

"Don't hold your breath, dear."

Kevin waited for Sophia to pick her stuff up, and they went home together. Upon arrival, she called her parents to tell them how much she loved them. The rain never stopped until late that night. The kids were sleeping, and while sitting by the window in the kitchen, Kevin and Sophia started talking while sipping some hot chocolate. They reminisced about how life used to be in their separate homes, what they liked to eat and drink, the places they visited, the things their respective families used to do together, their misdeeds, and what they dreamed of becoming when they grew up—But time had gone by so fast. Now they were adults with kids, and responsibilities were upon their shoulders. As the rain let up, and with the conversation, the dark ideas were leaving Sophia's head. Her imagination turned into more enjoyable things. She kept dreaming, but some dreams can never be fully described, let alone fulfilled. She had to accept the fact that some of the craziest dreams sometime do come true. It is worth dreaming. It is worth being proactive. It is worth holding on to one's values. She turned on her computer; there was another email from Dad.

Dear Sophia:

My beloved daughter, why abandon the good habits? As I am getting older, my traveling time is being reduced, so I decided to visit you with this email. Last night, your mother and I were reviewing the various pictures in our albums. As the two of us reminisced, we realized how quickly time flies. It feels like just yesterday we thought we were going to be together forever. Now everyone is going their own way. I feel like I have come to the top of the mountain already. As I am thinking about you and your brother, I wanted to remind you of a few tips about parenting. I would like you not to make the same errors that your mother and I made while you and Junior were growing up.

1. Remember your priorities: God, your soulmate, your children, and then the rest.

2. Based on the current trends, you need to be vigilant and stay close to your kids. These are the most precious gifts from heaven. Spend time with them, be their confidant, take part in all their activities, and never miss one opportunity to remind them of your love for them. Give them the best education possible. Raise them with discipline, firmness and tact. Remember your examples are more persuasive than all the speeches in the world. Here are a few tips in raising children:

a. Parents can form the destiny of the children through training, modeling, and guidance. The best way is—after teaching them about values, ethics, right and wrong, good and bad—through examples, lifestyle, and commitment. Be consistent, not irrational, or irritable, or unpredictable or possessive.

b. *Everyone and everything in the children's surroundings has an impact on them including their mother and father, brothers and sisters, grandparents, babysitters, schools, teachers, colleges, and the type of interactions between them and other individuals and things. These will affect their self-esteem, self-worth, and self-actualization. So be careful where you place them and what they are exposed to through their senses. Be a good friend, and beware of peer pressure and bad influences of some friends, who do not have their best interests in mind; they do not know any better. So be there.*

c. *No one can live without discipline, obedience, a sense of purpose, and a sense of responsibility. Teach the kids about the consequences of every choice in life. Do not discipline with anger or out of frustration. Always remind them of your love even during the process of discipline.*

d. *Beware of causes that may trigger misbehavior such as a brain injury, peer pressure, the use of drugs, different types of abuse, general medicinal problems, personality, character, and unusual tendencies.*

e. *Invest quality time in interacting with them. Before you know it they will be grown up, with different agendas. Spend time interacting with them while they are growing up. Overall they prefer quality time rather than various material possessions. Develop and cultivate some great habits in them and with them: sharing meal times, spirituality, ethics, etiquette, a sense of responsibility, time management, respect, discipline, and integrity.*

f. *Remember that no one is perfect. Even the perfect God could not force Adam not to rebel against him. So do your best. But give them permission to fall, fail, and learn. When they fall, do not step on them; help them get up, build them up, and encourage them. Remember, with freedom there is always a risk of making the wrong choice but teach them there is a price for every choice. People have to pay the consequences of their actions.*

g. *Keep life simple, enjoyable, with the least stress possible, and instill a sense of purpose in them. Remember, children may have the same parents, but each one is different and needs to be dealt with accordingly; each one deserves specially tailored attention based on his needs.*

As Mom and I are together, we still think about you guys; you are still very dear to us and we wanted to let you know how much we love you and miss you and the kids. But life goes on. So be good, be of good courage, and may God bless you all!

Love,

Dad

Case Studies

Sophia, Kevin, Bertha, Bernard, Junior, Lakisha. Brenda, and Marvin represent no specific person that you know, but any or all of them could be any one of us. Do not attempt to match any of these characters with anyone you know. They are used just to make the various points easier to grasp. The main purpose is to illustrate the various situations, conditions, trials, and struggles of life on this planet. In order to widen the range of possibilities and increase the chance that you can identify yourself with any of the examples, here are a few practical cases.

CASE #1

Joan and Paul met at a social gathering. They fell madly in love with each other. Paul felt as if he could not live away from Joan. So he proposed, she accepted, and shortly after, they got married. The conjugal life was great, except for one problem: Paul was getting increasingly jealous, to the point Joan was thinking about getting out of the relationship. What could be done?

We do not know how long the love relationship lasted before they got married. Maybe Paul manifested his jealousy before marriage. It would be helpful to find out how he used to behave before marriage. If he was as possessive before as he was after, we would like to determine whether or not Joan was among those who fall into the trap of thinking they can change their partners once they get married. It never works. After marriage, the masks are thrown away, and people are seen for who they really are. The situation may even get worse with time. Assuming neither partner is giving the other reasons to be jealous (being flirtatious, receiving strange private phone calls, unexplained disappearances, or other actions or behaviors that are suspicious), this can be a serious situation.

When two people fall in love, they want to be inseparable. They would love to share each other's company at all times and even want to raise a wall around or a sign on the forehead of the beloved to keep everyone else away. However, the practical aspects of life make such a desire impossible to be fulfilled. So mature people learn to adjust and develop certain attributes to keep them going even when away from each other. The two lovebirds must be able to invest some trust in that relationship and not attempt to take away the other's freedom to live his or her life as a balanced person. When someone becomes obsessively jealous and beyond reason, it becomes toxic and may strangle that specific love he or she wants to preserve. Normally everyone has a little dose of jealousy, even in the background. This is why each partner needs to be candid, truthful, and trustworthy. When jealousy becomes pathological, that is, when the other person is constantly under surveillance, being accused, or even embarrassed; the couple must seek professional counseling before it turns into a tragedy.

Here are five steps to take to avoid feeding the flame of jealousy:

1. Keep the lines of communication open and let your partner know about your daily schedule and activities—not the little details, necessarily—but

the essentials of your whereabouts: 9–5 at work, then hairstylist, or going to see someone in the hospital, school, conference…

2. Watch your outfits going to work and office parties; avoid giving the wrong message through your clothing and conversation, and avoid bringing someone's name (from work) up over and over, and do not let a co-worker answer your cell phone for you, especially when your partner is calling.

When at home, be there physically as well as mentally. Show attention, dedication, and appreciation.

3. Avoid frequent phone calls from people unknown to the partner and avoid secretive, private calls at home.

4. Try to get your partner to know your friends as much as it is possible.

5. Do not disappear for weeks or even days unless it is a scheduled, verifiable conference that goes with your profession. If the partner wants to go with you, if possible, let him or her come.

Case #2

Martine loves Joseph very much. She cannot imagine living without him. Yet, whenever they get together, Joseph never fails to make her feel guilty, devalued, and shameful. Martine says flatly, "Joseph always winds up having it his way; I wish I could leave him, but I just don't feel I can."

Martine is agonizing about her feelings. She is unsure about what to do.

Does she really love him? The answer is most likely that she does but he is strangling that sentiment. Now, in this specific case, there seem to be two issues to address:

1. Is this domestic abuse? Remember, domestic abuse refers to physical or emotional abuse between spouses, cohabitants, and non-married intimate partners; it can also include abuse and violence during dating and courtship. Does this represent symptoms of an abusive relationship?

2. Is this a manipulation technique used by one partner in order to control, manipulate, or get the other one to do what the former wants him or her to do at all time? Is he manipulative, does he make bad jokes about you; and is he jealous and possessive?

In both cases, you need to step back, become fully aware about what is going on, return to your base line—your values—and take the appropriate steps to establish yourself on better footing. He or she has to comply or face the consequences. If therapy is needed, or if legal intervention is required, take the necessary steps to protect your sanity and stay alive. Do not get into the self-doubt and self-blame emotions and let the situation get out of hand. Emotional abuse can have long psychological, physical, economic, and social effects. It is paramount that the counselor chosen shares your values, culture, and beliefs.

Case #3

Sasha places a frantic call to her pastor the fourth night of her honeymoon. She is really concerned about Vladimir, who behaves like an animal. All he ever wants is sex. She is really disappointed. She wants to leave and go home to her parents. This is an important issue that tends to be neglected because of the new trends in this world. The fact of the matter is before getting married, both man and woman must learn about each other's differences and also how to have a great but compatible and mutually enjoyable sexual relationship. She should know how men prioritize sexual intimacy. He should know how women care about affection, foreplay, and emotional connections. The gentleman must know the steps, the foreplay, the basic approach, and how to make it mutually enjoyable. So the man should be considerate enough, while the woman should do her best to accommodate. The best way is mutual consent and desire. It is not inappropriate to mention the possibility of having the same couple years later talking about boredom even in their sex lives. The key is to keep finding ways to improve the relationship in and out of the bedroom, recognize the changes that are bound to happen, and learn the various ways to keep the fire burning by adding a little surprise here and there, spending time together, etc.

Case #4

Linda and John have been married for almost six months. They are considered by many as new in the conjugal life; nevertheless, both of them seem disappointed. Their main problems: frequent arguments, disillusionment, frustration, deceptions. What should they do?

It is safe to say this is a common phenomenon. People get all excited, all psyched up for a great marriage, have great honeymoon, and a life filled with love, peace, joy, success, financial security, and stability, and expect to live happily ever after. In real life, nothing is further from the truth. In some cases, right before and even during the wedding ceremony or shortly after, the conflicts start and they may increase first before they decrease. Why? Because of our nature, we are free, autonomous, and intelligent beings. Based on our background, experiences, and genetics, we tend to see things in a certain way. Our tastes, visions, beliefs, cultures, and emotions all are somewhat different. If our personalities do not allow us to compromise, things can really get out of hand.

But as a general rule, all families encounter problems. Since the couple should price their commitment to each other above all, they look for ways to resolve conflicts:

1. Acknowledge the problem and define it—the type and the extent.

2. Identify the source, the causes, and the motifs that make the problem come up, if possible.

3. Evaluate your role in such a problem.

4. Decide to solve it once it appears instead of pushing it under the rug. Don't just talk it out. Act on it; make changes. Show genuine desire and action to have it taken care of.

5. Once it is solved, do not bring it back up when dealing with another one. There will be plenty to deal with, so do not dwell on the past; learn from it.

6. Watch your words and body language. Speak respectfully to each other and not both at the same time. Modulate the tone of voice, and filter the words used. Give solid reason for your position. Do not corner the partner or make him or her feel defenseless, guilty, and ashamed.

7. Learn to compromise and learn how and when (if at all) to pick a fight.

Another cause for disappointment is the fact that after marriage, people let their guard down or they want to change or mold the other partner. Let it be clear: take him as he is, love her for herself. Learn how to grow together by spending time with each other. Keep working at the relationship, and never take it for granted.

Another reason for disillusionment is that some people believe when they are married there is no room for privacy or secrecy. Let us be clear about it. Everyone needs some space to breathe. Give your partner some space. A well-balanced person makes the crucial decision as to what in his or her past to reveal or not to reveal. Whatever can affect the couple's life should be known. For example, a young man may tell a woman, *I can only marry someone who is a virgin. Otherwise, her life with me is going to be hell.* The young woman he is crazy about should find the proper time and place to tell him if she is not a virgin. She has no obligation to tell him how many men before him, or how many times. If a partner has a sexually transmitted disease, he or she should tell the other partner. The bottom line is you want to have a clear conscience by revealing what directly concerns the other person and may affect the relationship. Furthermore, there are certain things that can be said up front; others can come along as time goes by and the two people trust each other more. Otherwise, you risk divulging a deep secret that can become known to many other people you did not want to know about.

C<small>ASE</small>#5

Marlene and Steven have been together for years. They look like two pigeons in love. Lately, Steven had noticed that Marlene has been very distant, not interacting, restless, unable to sleep, and even crying for almost no real reason. She is always tired, disorganized, has no energy to do anything but to stay in bed or watch TV passively. She does not want to go out or even receive visits. Steven is upset, and does not seem to know what to do?

It is not impossible for people in a long-term relationship, especially when they are getting old, to notice some changes. So what can be done?

1. If it is not because of a sudden change such as death, emptiness syndrome, or malnutrition, the other partner must make sure he or she is not the cause of those changes on account of mistreatment, subtle or obvious. In other words, when changes happen, the concerned partners cannot just assume. The situation must be examined to find the underlying cause.

2. The best bet is to convince the partner to seek medical help for an appropriate workup to identify depression, metabolic abnormalities, a tumor, or dementia.

3. When the cause or causes are identified, one needs to evaluate all options and find the proper course to take.

Case #6

Juliet and Gilbert got married. Soon after, she found out that Gilbert was a divorced man, had two teenagers from his previous marriage, and wanted to bring them to his new home. Juliet was upset. Gilbert claimed he did not want to lose her and that is why he did not tell her before. She was not quite sure about what to do.

In this day and age, step-parents and step children have become more and more a condition to be reckoned with. In this particular situation, Gilbert started out on the wrong foot. He did not tell his spouse about those children. One cannot keep a secret if it is going to affect the couple's life. We wonder how Juliet happened to marry a man not knowing he was married before and had children. How many more secrets is such a couple hiding from each other? When entering into a relationship that requires a lifetime commitment, such as marriage, honesty is the best policy. Hiding the truth does not make it easier. Sooner or later the truth will come out. Then, for not being forthcoming, you will lose that partner's trust, which will be very hard to gain back.

This relationship is very complicated: sharing a life with a partner who cannot be trusted and children who are not yours. How do we make life possible in such a house?

Based on her religious beliefs regarding living with a previously divorced man, her values, and her viewpoint about love, trust and commitment, she may decide to find out more about that previous marriage, accept him, or send him home packing. But it is a personal decision with all the consequences. Assuming they are living together, here are a few steps that should be taken:

1. Learn to be fair, realizing the kids are not responsible for the situation, and make them feel at home.

2. Show them you are interested in them and their well-being, you are there for them, and they can talk to you and convey their worries and problems.

3. Based on their ages, be patient and realize that they may resent you. They already have habits and manners contracted from their former home.

4. Set some basic rules about boundaries and what is acceptable and what is not.

5. Set limits and obey them yourself.

6. Tell them about rights and responsibilities. If Juliet has children of her own, or if Gilbert and Juliet have children together, this makes the situation even more complicated. At any rate, avoid showing favoritism; try to convey as much fairness as possible.

7. Try not to be the missing parent; they will never accept you as such.

8. Try to be a friend, be sincere, and respect their decisions.

Case #7

Nancy and Jeff have been married for twenty years. Their two kids are in college. The day after Christmas, Nancy hands Jeff divorce papers. Se tells him she does not love him anymore, and she wants out of the relationship. It is a devastating blow to Jeff. It takes him weeks to realize it is real. He begs, and even promises to do anything to save the relationship. Nancy does not budge. She moves out of the house and goes to live with her sister temporarily. Everybody is up in arms. No one can explain what happened. Blame, guilt, and accusations are flying back and forth. What a disaster! Obviously, this did not happen overnight. There had been precedents, warning signs that were never addressed. Let us quickly point out ten core principles for a successful marriage:

1. Unwavering commitment to the marriage vows, the institution as a covenant that supersedes the individuals involved in such an engagement.

2. Commitment to cultivate a selfless, unconditional love for the partner, even in allowing him or her to fail sometimes. Give him or her room to breathe. Remember you can commit yourself to love someone but you may not be in love with that person all the time. Every now and then he or she will do something that will get under your skin. But your overall love will stick around long enough to forgive and move on. This is why the

partner is strongly advised to be ingenious and to discover tips and secrets to keep romance in the relationship.

3. Commitment to work incessantly at improving the relationship. Make it your top priority through the various aspects of life. Be vigilant, and watch for signs. Never take the partner for granted.

4. Commitment to dedicate time to the relationship and to treat the partner as the most important person in your life.

5. Commitment to appreciate and respect the partner.

6. Commitment to always keep the ways of communications open and to have meaningful dialogue and nip any differences in the bud.

7. Commitment to accept the partner's imperfections, to forgive, forget, and counsel.

8. Commitment to pay attention to the partner in every little detail through calls, gifts, compliments, and enjoyable surprises.

9. Commitment to be sympathetic and available in times of trial of the spouse and family members. When the storm hits, the partner needs to be able to count on you.

10. Commitment to maintain a positive attitude, have a sense of humor, to be grateful and helpful, and never be a burden, a source of stress, or add fire to any flames.

Even after practicing all these, you may still be vulnerable if the partner decides to leave you. After all, the first reason for divorce is to have been married. But you will have a clear conscience and you can be sure he or she will not find someone like you.

<u>Case #8</u>

Debbie and David were married for seven years before they had children. Then they were blessed with two adorable children, Hans and Barbara, within three years. Everybody was very happy for them, but they were facing critical challenges. They were getting on each other's nerves. Every little thing was becoming a federal case. Not too long ago, David informed Debbie he wanted some space. He needed some time to think. Debbie got very angry and told him not to bother coming back, ever. "I'll have one less child to deal with!" she screamed at David over the phone. What can they do to save their marriage? After seven years of enjoying each other with an uninterrupted honeymoon, the freedom to go anywhere and do anything, having two babies in three years caused serious changes, if not disruption, in the couple's life. The children consumed all the parents' energy and there was none left for each other. They needed a timeout. Consider the situation. Instead of blaming each other or getting on each other's nerves, the couple needs to go back to the drawing board. What do they have going for them? The children should cement their love and not break it. They need to seek competent counseling for time management, stress management, and conflict resolution. Mom and Dad must take turns and share responsibilities for their children, and allocate precious time for each other. When the tank is empty, it needs to be filled. The couple has other challenges waiting for them in raising the kids to be decent citizens. They must act as a team with a common goal, dissolve their frustrations, and avoid built up, and spilled over resentment. The initial step is whether or not both of them want to work on their marriage. The sooner the better, before any third party complication sets in.

CASE #9

Denise and Richard appear to be a lovely couple. Apparently, they were made for each other. They just counted their eleventh year of marriage. Denise tells Richard she can no longer pretend. She just does not love him. She never did. Richard himself admits he no longer feels anything for her either. What has happened? Human beings are always searching for happiness, stability, and security. Therefore, we often tend to go for the obvious while neglecting what is more subtle. Richard was young, handsome, very popular, and athletic. He was loved by everyone. He was from a wealthy family and was doing fairly well in class. Denise was likely in love with that person; better yet, Denise's family was flattered that Richard would chose her among all the beautiful girls on campus. Now she is more mature. The dust has settled. The fame is forgotten. Richard and Denise are now facing each other. The result is not encouraging. When a couple decides they have had enough of each other, it is very difficult if not impossible to have them change their mind. So, it is very important that the foundation be solid. It cannot be just mere emotion or outside pressure, because in the long run, only the couple will suffer the bulk of disappointment in their life.

CASE #10

Melissa is thirteen, and Janice is sixteen. Both are growing up in a lovely family where Mom and Dad did their best to respond to all their needs in every aspect of life that is humanly possible. They are seen as angels and sweethearts, contrary to their older brother James, who was involved in all kinds of misdeeds and was known to be the rebellious type. Once Melissa turns thirteen she starts acting up. Shortly after, her sister Janice joins in. Together they make a pair of bandits. They seem to have conspired to reject everything they were taught by their parents. Their music, outfits, and hairstyles are scandalous, to say the least, for the parents. Not long ago, their school principals informed their parents that they had missed twenty days of schooling in three months. They are failing their classes. Almost daily, they wake up late, eat one thing or two, leave the dishes in the sink, and then disappear to go hang out with friends, or go to movies or concerts. In their rooms there is a collection of half-empty cans and bottles, unfinished sandwiches and snacks, with their clothes all over. To top it all off, they talk back; they do not listen to their parents anymore. The other night, they got home way past midnight and that was it. Their mother had to restrain their dad from physically hitting them. The parents want to take them and go out of state to a new environment. What do you do in a condition like this?

There is growing dissatisfaction among parents regarding the behavior of their children. The adolescent stage is a difficult time to deal with. There is no one magic approach for all. Every child and every home is different. Let us review the general principles.

1. Spend time interacting with the children daily. Do not spy on them, but find out from them what they are thinking. Be their friends. Show them you are always approachable for talking. They come first. Be open-minded. Never show them that any question can shock you. Take them out to parks, shows, concerts, the movie theater, and on other excursions.

2. Be alert. Do not spy on them; yet know what they are watching and where they go on the Internet. Do not leave them wandering on the school premises hours before or after school. Beware of the possibility of abuse even by people you would have never thought could do that. Do not blame others for your children in front of them. If you feel others did your kids wrong, go and handle it in their absence. Do not make them feel you are always going to stand by them and blame others for their misdeeds. For example, if you suspect some teachers were unjust, you go and handle it between you and the teacher. Do not disrespect adults in front of your kids for them. Be aware of the fact that your kids may lie; show them you trust them, yet keep your eyes open. Remember the best way to educate your children is by example.

3. Never fail to remind them of your values, ethics, beliefs, and the reasons for them. Be keen to know who their friends are. Have your home available for their friends to come instead of them going to unknown places doing unknown things. Have some disciplinary rules and some structure in the home.

Of course, none of this can guarantee the expected outcome, but be on the lookout. Often parents tend to be quiet when things are going right. They only react when things go wrong. No. Whatever happens, take time to congratulate the children. Build up their self-esteem, and their confidence; encourage them without giving them a superiority complex. Of course they will fail and fall. They will disappoint you. They will do things you never thought they were capable of. Haven't we all? But love them anyway. Help them to get up while paying the consequences. Let them know early there is a price to pay for every choice made in life. After all is said and done, pray, pray, and pray! Try to stay calm. Avoid projecting hatred toward your children instead of toward their actions. Try not to discipline on the spot, when you are upset, frustrated, and angry. Take a deep breath. Practice self-restraint. You will personally discover that raising children has also taught you a few lessons and has had some positive impact on how you manage stress and anger.

All in all, do your best. Never give up hope. Find a way to draw energy. You will need to refill your tank more often than you anticipate. Put your trust in a higher power as much as you can.

Suggested Protocol for a Lasting Relationship: Golden Rules

- Know yourself, who you are and what you want in life.

- Have realistic expectations in a relationship.

- Active personal selfless devotion to make it last.

- Set limits, define what is acceptable and what is not, define consequences and follow through.

- Continually reassess the status of the relationship.

- Acquire knowledge and steps for self-improvement.

- Beware of love killers: complaisance, boredom, resentment, and selfishness, lack of communication, financial difficulties, and unfaithfulness.

- Keep the romantic fire always burning.

- Allow breathing space and accept the partner as is.

- Identify the warning signs: neglect, boredom, recurrent argument, avoiding each other, lack of accountability, reluctance or lack of interest in discussing difficulties.

- Anticipate potential challenges, and know when counseling is needed and whom to choose as a counselor.

- Every couple has their own dynamic: avoid stereotyping.

- Weigh the impacts of sociocultural, behavioral, mental, physical, and spiritual aspects of life. Take a multidimensional approach.

Epilog

As you finish reading these pages, one or two things may have caught your attention. You may have laughed or frowned, or both; you may also wonder why I wrote a book on such a popular topic. Frankly speaking, I must admit it is because I see so many people unhappy in their relationships. Most of the time, they blame the other partner. The truth is, most people do not know the basics about keeping a healthy relationship going. I can say that all my life I have been an avid observer of human beings. In the city where I have spent most of my life, as well as in those that I have visited, I have seen all kinds of people: big and small, tall and short, black, yellow, white, affluent and poor, highly educated professionals and those who are barely surviving. One thing they all have in common is love. Love controls us all. It has a wide spectrum of manifestations. No matter what we have accomplished in life, we are nothing unless we have been conquered by love. As time passes by, if we ever look back, many of us wish we were a bit more loving to our partners. As the kids grow old and leave the nest, some family members may come for the holidays, some friends may visit in the hospital some mere strangers may perform an act of kindness, but everyone needs someone to love. Everyone needs to be truly loved. There will come a time, if we live long enough and if we remain lucid, that we will wish we had a significant other even just to argue with.

After all is said and done,
Long after we're all gone,
Love will still be around
With its glorious crown!
When we get old and grey,
When our memory
goes astray,
When we forget how
to pray,
Will they be there to play?

Selected Resources

It is humanly impossible to name all the books, and cite all the authors who have contributed to give birth to this book. I am likely going to omit some names, but it won't be intentional. Here is a partial list of the books and authors read for this book:

Cutrer, William, M.D., Glahn, Sandra.
Sexual Intimacy in Marriage.
Grand Rapids, MI: KREGEL PUBLICATIONS, 1998, 2001

Dobson, James.
Marriage Under Fire.
Sisters, OR: MULTNOMAH PUBLISHERS, INC., 2004

Hagee, John & Diana.
What Every Man Wants in a Woman; What Every Woman Wants in a Man.
Lake Mary, FL: CHARISMA HOUSE, 2005

Lepine, Bob.
The Christian Husband.
Ventura, CA: REGAL BOOKS, 1999

Lewis, Robert and Hendricks, William.
Rocking the Roles.
Colorado Springs, CO, NAVPRESS, 1991, 1998

Munroe, Myles.
The Purpose and Power of Love & Marriage.
Shippensburg, PA: DESTINY IMAGE PUBLISHERS, INC., 2002

Drs. Parrott, Les & Leslie.
The Love List.
Grand Rapids, MI: Zondervan, 2002

Parson, Rob.
The Sixty Minute Marriage.
Nashville, TN: Broadman & Holman Publishers, 1998, 2001

Rainey, Dennis & Barbara.
The New Building Your Mate's Self-Esteem.
Nashville, TN: Thomas Nelson, Inc., 1995

Rainey, Dennis & Barbara.
Rekindling the Romance.
Nashville, TN: Thomas Nelson, Inc., 2004

Sande, Ken.
Peacemaking for Families.
Wheaton, IL: Tyndale House Publishers, 2002

Self, Carolyn Shealy and William L.
Survival Kit for Marriage.
Nampa, ID: Pacific Press Publishing Association, 1998

Smalley, Gary.
Making *Love Last Forever.*
Dallas, TX: Word Publishing, 1996.

Vaudré, P. Jacques.
Six Dynamic Keys to an Effective Marital Covenant Love Relationship. Montreal, Canada, 2001

Quick Order Form

Email orders: **Jfranc6704@aol.com**

Fax orders to: **718-531-2329**

Call for order at: **718-531-6100** Have your credit card ready.

Mail in orders at:

Jean D. François, MD
P.O. Box 360543
Brooklyn NY 11236

Please send the following Books, CD, reports:

I am interested in:

☐ Speaking/ seminars/conferences

☐ Consulting

☐ Other services needed (Please specify):_____

_____

Name: _____

Address: _____

City:_____State: _____ Zip: _____

Telephone: _____

Cell #: _____

Email address: _____

Shipping and handling:

U.S.: $5.00 for first book, $2.00 for each additional.

www.ingramcontent.com/pod-product-compliance
Lightning Source LLC
Chambersburg PA
CBHW071452040426
42444CB00008B/1306